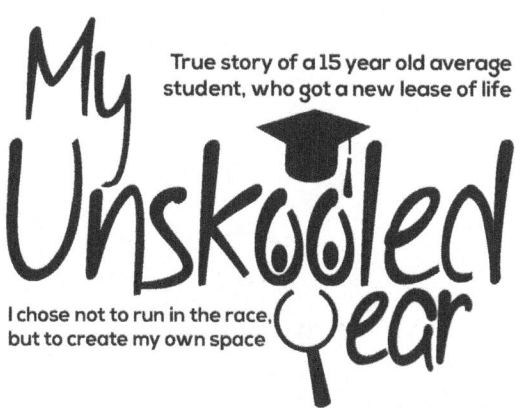

My Unskooled Year

True story of a 15 year old average student, who got a new lease of life

I chose not to run in the race, but to create my own space

Sagarikka

notionpress.com

Notion Press

Old No. 38, New No. 6
McNichols Road, Chetpet
Chennai - 600 031

First Published by Notion Press 2016

ISBN 978-1-946048-79-0

This book is dedicated to my grandfather
Dr. V.A. Sathgurunath, who was always independent and tireless.
He taught me the importance of planning and has
always been a source of information for me.
Also my grandmother Mrs. Bala Sathgurunath who has always
showered her love and blessings on me unconditionally.

TESTIMONIALS

- An educational experiment

  Sagarikka Sivakumar says she learned more about the world after she took a break from senior school – ***The Hindu July 22, 2016***

- This 16-year-old quit high school to explore life and her journey will inspire you

  While the Delhi University cut-off marks are turning the dreams of many student upside down in northern India, down south, in Tamil Nadu, is a girl who decided to take a break after finishing her tenth grade, quit school for a year to explore life and guess what? She is all set to publish a book called 'My Unskooled Year' – ***India Today July 1, 2016***

- Remarkable – a 16 year old who dropped out of school for a year & wrote a book about what she learned out of school – ***Tweeted by Sashi Tharoor @SashiTharoor***

- Unschooling the mind – while many teenagers find themselves at a confusing juncture of career paths after class 10, 16 year old Sagarikka took the road not taken. – ***Deccan Chronicle Aug 5th, 2016.***

CONTENTS

FOREWORD

Wow! And wow again. What extraordinary parents. What an extraordinary child. What an extraordinary journey.

In the West the concept of taking a gap year sometime during your academic tenure is common, but not so in India. In India, parents are focussed on just one thing for their wards. Studies. It is the straight and narrow path to everything. And so children tread this cookie cutter path, surrendering their talents, their dreams and passions in order to become managers, doctors and engineers.

In college, my best friend had two angelic brothers, twins, who were near geniuses in art. Even in school, they used to produce detailed and beautifully drawn comic books. It almost broke my heart when I met them a few years later to find that these tender hearted lads had now been groomed for the corporate rat race.

Thank goodness for Savitri and Siva! And for others of their ilk. Parents who are willing to challenge the prevailing mind set, to step off the treadmill, to invest time in their child, to refuse to give up on her when she gets less than ideal marks in her 10th standard, but who, at the same time, open up the world for her in the course of what Sagarrika calls her Unskooled Year (USY). The couple orchestrated a fantastic learning experience that included a highly disciplined schedule (waking up at 6.30 am and keeping at it till 10 pm), selling Amway products, going to various places of work including a hotel, hospital, bank and BPO and writing up her experiences every single day. There was travelling to Mount Kailash and Leh, there was attending many conferences and events, there was meeting thousands of inspiring people, there was exposure to different industries including an NGO, and several other things besides.

Indeed, reading through her enriching narrative, I, at 59, feel positively dwarfed. I have not had half the exposure she got during this one year, or the many opportunities she got to understand how money, business and science work. I can barely even comprehend what kind of a girl she will turn out to be and what kind of a future she will have. As her parents said in one of their many notes in the book, they wanted their daughter to be focussed on possibilities. As far as I can see, Sagarrika today has access to innumerable opportunities. She has already realised more than most of us would in a lifetime. She has started a blog, made a couple of documentaries, and hello, she has written this book!

I thoroughly enjoyed reading this book, written in a straightforward yet engaging way by this novice writer. Even at this age, her personality clearly shines, a droll sense of humour, a certain confidence, a wonderful capacity to organise her experiences simply but clearly, and to always get the lesson. She has passed on the many words of wisdom she was imparted, and the reader is the better for it.

I do hope her book, and the person she became during the course of her USY, will inspire other parents to let their children off their leash and allow them to explore life and themselves before deciding what they intend to devote the rest of their lives to.

Life is so much more than a pay cheque or a pension. Life is beautiful and exciting and each of us has come down to Planet Earth with a brief to enrich it in our own unique ways. As the Editor of Life Positive, I meet people almost on an everyday basis who tell me how they left their jobs as Chartered Accountants, Corporate Honchos or Bank Managers because they felt called to do something else. Many wound up as healers, therapists, trainers, artists or writers. How much easier it would have been for them had they been allowed to discover their inclinations at a younger age.

I have known Siva and Savitri for quite a while now, for they have attended quite a few of the Expos Life Positive has organised. Their commitment to their spiritual and personal growth is striking, and their devotion to each other inspiring. I commend this wonderful couple for their courageous and committed parenting, and eagerly look forward to Sagarikka's future progress.

— Suma Varghese, Editor, Life Positive

FOREWORD

Advices today pour in to parents of children in tenth and twelfth standards from all and sundry as to the importance of education and what that child should be. Everyone other than the child is consulted on the future choice of that child's education. The passion and creativity which takes shape in a child's mind over several years of school education and observation is forever crushed or put into cold storage. Anything spoken to parents and guardians in this regard is considered "out of syllabus" by several parents. In many a home today the crave for higher and higher marks by the parents and sometimes the peer puts an indomitable pressure on young minds; by sending them to coaching centres, some of which functioning as "rote jails" to produce "human robots" of no independent thinking and choice. Self concept deteriorating, most of these kids land up to know how to "earn" rather than how to "learn"... Amidst this chaos it is simply exalting to see the likes of Mrs and Mr Sivakumar who facilitated their child Sagarikka's desire to "explore" her passion for knowledge for a year before she self consciously decided what she should be... Is it one year wasted? or several years gained?

I am thrilled to go through this book by Sagarikka titled "*My Unskooled Year*" in short USY. It's all about her real "schooling" out of school. In fact I hastened to acknowledge writing a foreword to this book when we happened to meet as this is what I did to my daughter Azra when she wanted a break for a year after her tenth. A parent of one crazy girl (according to my colleagues), writing the foreword for the book penned by another "crazy" girl, who ventured to "learn" by experiencing and observing before continuing her higher education. Education is all about what a child can imbibe, as a learning process.

Brilliant observations of several kinds by Sagarikka classified into seven chapters followed by her conclusions; and suggesting do's and don'ts... makes a good reading. "Notes from parents" constitute a good guiding tool for the parents who should be reading this book.

After a brief introduction, Sagarikka's emphasis on discipline and time management paves the way to the success of her USY. Her business, travel and other experiences form beautiful sequels which provide first hand information of the learning process. Name the subject you study in class, she has used them during these sojourns. Mathematics, Commerce, Accountancy, Stock Marketing, Travel, Cinema, Climate, Temperature, Biological systems all became a practical training. Her meeting people of different specialties from different industries and professions appears to have given her the confidence to tackle challenging situations; which is reflected in pages concerning the accident the family met on the highway and her confident intervention.

I wish every child as well as every parent of school going kids read this book, and though, most of you may disagree for a year's break in study, at least give children an opportunity, whenever free, to interact, explore and learn from the society in which they are going to exist as future citizens of this great country... India.

My best wishes to Sagarikka and her parents and wish all readers an enjoyable reading... a journey through unskooled year.

— Mr. Sultan Ahmed Ismail

M.Sc., Ph.D., D, Sc, Soil Biologist and Ecologist

Positions Held:

Director
Ecoscience Research Foundation
Chennai 600041, India

Former Head
Department of Biotechnology
The New College
Chennai 600014, India

Research Director (Honorary)
Dr MGR Janaki College
Chennai 600028, India

Head, Department of Zoology and
Vice Principal, The New College
Chennai 600 014, India

Director, Institute of Research in
Soil Biology and Biotechnology
The New College
Chennai 600014, India

PREFACE

This book is the outcome of the constant guidance, love and encouragement provided to me by many people.

For every step I took I was mentored and guided by my parents Ms. Savitri and Mr. Sivakumar. Even for projects and the trip to Leh, my parents had complete faith and confidence in me and gave me the freedom to experiment. They planned out my projects, my industrial visits, my trips, my seminars, my classes and even went to the extent of fixing appointment to meet people. So in some portions of the book I have mentioned that they are Mrs. and Mr. Architect of my life.

I wish to thank my Aunt Ms. Deepa Natarajan, Mrs. Owenita D'Cruz, Mrs. Nirmala Varier and Mr. S. Sivanandan for going through every line of my book and making innumerable corrections. But for them I don't think this book would have been readable.

I thank members of the staff of TRICHY PLUS (my Dad's company) for their support. A special thanks to Ms. Parsha bi for helping me with the layout of the book. I also thank Ms. Indhuja Raghavan from Bengaluru for her support in designing the initial book cover.

Finally, I wish to thank the Google Dictionary for giving me the apt words and the synonyms which helped me in communicating with my readers.

ACKNOWLEDGEMENT

My special thanks to all the wonderful individuals who believed in me, instilled confidence in me and made "My Unskooled Year" dream become a reality.

INTRODUCTION

8.2! My grade stared at me on the face. I was at the bottom half of my class in the tenth standard Central Board Secondary Examination.

My parents are trainers and teachers. They run an institute in Trichy, Tamil Nadu and coach students for entrance exams. My dad is a fun loving person. Though, he is very serious at work, we have pillow fights at home. My mother is a very calm lady and encourages me all the time. I have had the best childhood. My parents have always smothered me with kisses.

Till my 10th, there was one thing I liked to do. Dance! I would attend all dance competitions and win many prizes. Dancing helped me stay away from school most of the time. I would not have to attend classes as I would either be practicing or participating in competitions. I also liked to play. I would play in the evenings while my friends would attend tuitions. However my parents never forced me to attend any of these classes. I have a lot of friends and many of them are college students. My way of expressing affection to them was to slap them on their back, pull their ear and punch them in their stomach. They would tolerate me because dad and mom were their teachers. They would buy me chocolates and take me to cake shops. Life was fun.

Whenever it rained, I would dance to my heart's content and get drenched to the bones. I would also go with my dad on a two-wheeler and shout till my lungs were about to burst. All this was about to change.

It all started two months before my tenth exam. All of a sudden, my friends, relatives and neighbours, started asking me about my preparation. A sudden realisation came upon me that this exam was something very important. It would change the course of my life. One particular day, my relatives, my grandfather, grandmother, grandmother's sister and an uncle called me for a serious discussion. They told me that if only I get good marks in 10th, would I be able to opt for Science group... Only if I got Science group, would I get into engineering or medicine... And only if I got engineering or medicine, would I get a good job... Then only could I be happy in life. They also scolded my parents and said that they were responsible for my immaturity. They urged me to grow up.

I could not sleep that night. I was really worried. There were only two months left for the board exam. My grandmother started doing Sathya Narayana pooja for my success. She offered to break 108 coconuts to Lord Vinayaka and also put vadamala for Lord Hanuman. Now I had to score good marks not only for myself, but to also keep all my well-wishers happy.

My preparation was like that of a cricket team, who did not score in the first 40 overs and tried to make up for the loss in the last 10 overs. Unfortunately in the process they lose many wickets. I started my preparation in January. Every chapter was like Greek and Latin to me. My father helped me with Maths and Science and my mother, with English and Social Studies. I tried to learn the problems, subjects and terms by heart, but my memory kept failing me. Somehow, I vomited whatever little I knew in the exam. Now it was up to God. I hoped that the coconuts and vadamala would do the job. After all, I am a very kind and loving person. Surely, the Gods wouldn't let me down!?

Then the tsunami struck on the day of the results. I hadn't received so many calls ever in my life. Everybody wanted to know how much I had scored. It dawned on me that this result was the most important event in my life. I wanted to melt away and vanish. Every time anyone asked me for my score, I would give a sad look, put my head down and whisper my score. Then people would console me as if a great tragedy had struck my life.

People are boring. They always have four standard questions to ask:

What is your name?

Which class are you studying in?

How many marks did you score?

What are your future plans?

Everyone... Same questions. I was getting tired. I thought of hanging a placard around my neck which would read as follows:

My name is Sagarikka.

I just completed my 10th standard.

My score is 8.2 CGPA.

My future? God only knows.

I remember that day quite vividly. My results came in the middle of May 2015. I was confused and worried. I had a discussion with my best friends. Most of my best friends had chosen Science group. Subi wanted to be a doctor. Hari wanted to be a computer engineer. Alfred told me that his parents had decided to make him an IAS officer. Anjana wanted to study Commerce. Everybody knew what to do. All of them were very clear about their future and I had no idea. I was not even sure of the spelling of Commerce. I was not aware of what they do in Commerce. I never wanted to be a doctor. I hated thrusting needle on people's backs. I had never enjoyed Maths and Science. I was confused about my future.

The next day, I sat with my parents at the dinner table. They smiled at me. I was very upset with them. They never scolded me for my poor marks. They only said "Well done". They never gave me any advice on what I should do in future. I looked at my dad and the conversation went like this.

Myself: Dad! What should I do? Which group should I take?

Dad: What do you want to do?

Myself: How do I know? I'm just a little child. I only know that I don't want to be a doctor. You have a lot of experience. You should tell me what to do.

Dad: What would you like to be?

Myself: Dad, I like robots. I had gone for a robotic workshop at NIT. I like dramatics (I had won at a State level drama competition in Chennai). I would like to be a dancer. I am the best dancer in my school. I would like to participate in team activities (I had won the title Ms. RYLA – Rotary Youth Leadership Award).

Dad: Then decide what you want.

I was getting irritated. I wished my parents were like other parents. I wished at least my mother would say something. She kept smiling all the time. Did they not realise that I was too young to decide? Then my mother spoke. What she said still rings in my ears.

Mom: Pappu (My nickname), would you like to explore for one year before you decide what you want to do?

Did I hear that right? One year to decide. Decide what? How?

Dad: We have a plan for you. Either you could follow our plan and explore the world for one year and decide what to do at the end of the year or join a group and go to school right away.

Who would say no to this proposal? One year of no school. One year of no homework. One year of no exams. I wanted to scream and dance in joy. Then dad spoke again.

Dad: But, under one condition, you should do exactly as we say!

I instantly agreed. I was ready for any terms and conditions and that is when the exciting journey of my UNSKOOLED YEAR (USY) began.

DISCIPLINE AND TIME MANAGEMENT

My idea of time management is limited to the stories about Mahatma Gandhi and his strict daily schedule. One story in particular impressed me. Gandhiji used to say his prayers everyday at 5am. He disliked tardiness and did not spare even a young girl. The girl came late because she had to comb and plait her long hair. Gandhiji sent her a pair of scissors.

The reason I have taken 'time management and discipline' as my first topic is I realise that without discipline my USY project would not have been a success.

Till then, I was a case study for discipline, and not a good one at that: Sleep! I could beat Kumbhakarna in this activity. On a normal day, I would sleep for ten hours. Usually I would wake up 20 minutes before the school bus came. Like the climax scene of a Bollywood movie, I would rush to catch the school bus. I have missed the bus many times and gone to school by auto. I was well known for standing outside the school gate when the assembly took place. Even today, my mother scolds me for not making the bed after waking up.

I had seen a beautiful video demonstration on time management. The trainer brought a jar, some sand, few small pebbles and some big stones. He asked the members of the audience to fill the jar with these things. One of them put the sand in first and then the pebbles. In the end, there was no room for the big stones. The trainer then did something amazing. He first put the big stones in. This created a lot of gap. He then put in the pebbles which filled up these large gaps. He then poured in the sand which filled up the smaller gaps. Now the jar was full. This created a deep impact in my mind. It taught me to do the important thing first and the least important thing last.

I had always been pouring in the sand. First I would watch countless movies a week, my favourite TV shows like Indian Idol, Britain's Got Talent and all IPL matches. Then I would put the pebbles in... my homework and assignments. The big stones were the last to go into my jar. I had never focused on understanding the subjects and learning new concepts.

How was I going to discipline myself for the next one year? Looking back, it seems like a miracle. I think the only reason I succeeded in my USY was because I wanted to prove something to the world which had given up on me.

My parents sat down with me and we worked out a time schedule for the next 12 months.

6.30 am: Wake up time.

7.00 am to 8.00 am: Fitness time. It was time for me to exercise and strengthen myself physically

8.15 am to 9.00 am: Reading the newspapers and learning new words.

9.30 am to 1.30 pm: Business experience, field visits and experiences at the stock market.

2.00 pm to 4.00 pm: Computer class.

4.30 pm to 5.30 pm: Playing badminton or sell products.

6.00 pm to 9.30 pm: Learning Science and Math with my dad.

10.00 pm to 10.45 pm: Reading and sharing experiences with family.

11.00 pm to 12.00: Relaxation time.

Weekends: Music, dance and SAT (Scholastic Aptitude Test) classes. Once a week: Go out for dinner and watch a movie.

Initially the going was very tough but I was committed to my schedule. 12 months into this journey, I cannot think of a life without discipline. My journey has just begun.

Notes from the parents:

We are the parents of Sagarikka (Pappu) our only child. We didn't have the privilege of having half a dozen kids like our grandparents. With half a dozen, the law of averages would always work. Some would click and some wouldn't.

In our case, we had to develop a system by which we could bring out the best in Sagarikka.

As avid readers, we had been impressed with the writings of Osho, who vehemently stated that, children should be like animals till the age of ten, uninfluenced by *social conditioning*. We had deliberately tried our best to bring Pappu up, devoid of *social conditionings*.

The analogy of Lord Krishna on the cover of 'Bhagwad Gita' caught up with us – parents should be like the charioteer Krishna, knowing when to pull the reins of the horse and when to let them go, thus bringing the fullest potential of the horse. We don't mean to say, bring up children like horses, but it was just to prove the point.

With fear and trepidation, we let Pappu go on the 'Unskooled Year' path. Many a time we had to give Pappu a sense of direction and be very cautious not to tread on her dreams. Every chapter will be ensued by our thoughts, fears and excitement.

We welcome suggestions in order to bring the best out of our child and also many other children, who are pursuing their dreams.

BUSINESS EXPERIENCE

- ALL ABOUT MONEY
- BUSINESS EXPERIENCES

ALL ABOUT MONEY

My first experience with money and business was with my dance team. I have participated in many dance shows with my team, in and out of Trichy. As my USY project was taking off, my dance team asked me to come for a dance show in Theni (200 kilometres from Trichy). I had already committed myself to my project, so I refused to accompany them. The head of the team tried to convince me to join them but, I firmly said no. I felt very good when I said 'NO'. The head called me again and promised to pay me Rs.2000 if I perform. Rs.2000! My head started to spin. I had done many dance shows and never was I paid a single paisa. And here for the first time, I was saying NO and they were ready to offer me Rs.2000.

I then started convincing my parents about how badly I wanted to get a feel of earning money. Mom did not appreciate me going to Theni for a day. She said that I would be breaking my word and my responsibility towards my USY. I coaxed and cajoled my parents. I told them that, this would be the last time that I would do such a program and they could count on me. They told me that it was my choice. So, off I went to Theni against their wishes. I did perform, one piece after the other in front of an uninterested audience. There were a few boys sitting in front, who kept whistling and ogling at our team of girls. It was a thoroughly irritating experience, but, the thought of Rs.2000 kept me going.

Now... was I paid for my performance? Till date I am yet to see the first rupee of the two thousand rupees.

My next experience with money came via M-L-M (Multi-Level Marketing). My parents had once been leading distributors of Amway products and had reached the level of Platinum. My dad believes that selling is one of the best experiences you can get in life and asked me to sell Amway products. I attended a training program to understand the products. I gathered that Amway has a lovely range of products. There is Nutrilite, which is a health care range. There is Personna, which is a personal care range, Artistry for beauty and the Amway home care range of products. The trainer explained each product, its features and advantages.

I went through the company website and got a lot of knowledge about the products.

I then went to the Amway pickup centre near my house and purchased products for Rs.20,000 (Mom's money, of course). I also picked up a lot of brochures. My parents gave me a list of 100 rich and successful people in town.

I was excited. I was sure all these 100 people would welcome me with open arms. They would give me lots of food to eat and then buy products worth at least Rs.5000 each. I was sure that some of them would buy products for even Rs.20,000 or Rs.30,000. I made a quick calculation. I imagined 100 people, all buying products for Rs.5000: I would have a turnover of over Rs.5,00,000 a month. My profit margin would be 35%- 40%. I would make at least Rs.2,00,000 per month.

What would I do with Rs.2,00,000 per month? In the first month, I would buy an iPhone and a DSLR camera. The next month I would buy an iMac and a Kindle reader. Then I would go for a Louis Vuitton bag and Alligator shoes. This would be soon followed by a Rolex watch. My wardrobe would be filled with designer dresses in the next six months. By the end of the year, I would have enough money to go on a trip to Disneyland.

My parents' best friends, such beautiful and environment friendly products, and an angel like me who would deliver these products; this was the best recipe to become a millionaire. I was sure I would be going to school the next year in a chauffeur driven Audi.

Then I hit a wall! I visited my mother's friend who is a very successful doctor. She told me that she was already buying Amway products from her daughter who is in the USA. I looked all around the house. I searched the bathrooms and cupboards but could not find a single Amway product in the house. I was seething with anger. Could she not buy at least one toothpaste or toothbrush to encourage me?

Then I met a top-notch lawyer. He scolded me, for wasting my life, trying to sell soap when I should have been studying. He told me that this was the time to focus on my education. I was extremely hurt.

He could have been kind and gently refused to buy the products. Why should I get scolding from a third person? Even my parents had never scolded me.

Each time I came home and shared these experiences with my parents, they would laugh and I would cry. It was a bad, bad world.

I also happened to meet a close friend of my father. He asked me not to sell my soul to an American company. He gave me a sermon on how MNCs are looting our country. He also suggested that I should be a true Indian. His mantra was, Make in India, Made in India. It's an irony that this uncle had lived for a good 20 years in Europe. Was he using 'Dabur Lal dant manjan' and 'Hajmola' there? Was he having 'Haldiram's Bhujia Sev' with his tea or drinking Bovonto Kalimark soda in Europe?

Later, I met the owner of a jewellery shop. She advised me against selling products made by others. She asked me to start my own manufacturing unit. I now had to contemplate on raising capital to start my own company.

I suddenly realised that the world is divided into two: Already Amway distributors and Swadeshis.

My task was to meet at least two people a week. Initially, I wanted to meet all the 100 in one day. Now meeting even two seemed to be a burden. My dad would motivate me every time saying that rejection is an opportunity to learn and handle objections. I was made to read Frank Bettger's book 'How I raised myself from failure to success in selling'.

Frank Bettger was initially a baseball player who was fired from his team. When he asked his manager why he was fired, he was told that he was not enthusiastic on the field. Frank Bettger took up the advice seriously. He decided to act enthusiastic even when he was not feeling enthusiastic and went on to become a successful baseball player.

I took the message earnestly and started acting enthusiastic.

Enthusiasm helped me to overcome my fear. Soon I was able to get a base of 15 customers. One of them, Uma aunty, the proprietor of PABCET College purchased products from me for Rs.5000 a month. Slowly I was able to generate a regular income of Rs.2000 to Rs.3000 from my Amway business.

What did I learn?

I learnt to overcome the fear of rejection and talk boldly to people.

I familiarised myself with record keeping. I kept records of the items purchased, items sold and the profit made.

I understood that follow up is very important in business. No customer called me up and told me that they required products. I had to regularly call them up and replenish the products.

This business gave me the confidence that I could stand on my own feet.

All said and done, selling was a very enjoyable experience.

Mandis, bazaars, medical representatives, call centres, insurance agents, stock brokers, mutual fund agents, advertisers, marketers, financial services, merchant bankers, politicians, writers, big retailers, street hawkers, movie and media barons, exclusive retailers, franchisees, dealers, distributors, schools, colleges and every professional under the sky… aren't they selling? Then why are people so negative about selling? Can somebody give me an answer?

My experience in the world of stock Market

For an entire month, I sat from 9 am till afternoon at a stockbroker's office. A dozen men, mostly in their mid 50s and 60s would come there every day. I would smile at everyone but they all looked very serious and were lost in their own world. I would notice some numbers running on the screen. These serious men would look at the screen like wolves waiting to pounce on their prey. All of a sudden, one of them would jump up in delight and I realised that this man had got his prey. The law of the jungle holds well in this world, the only difference being that this jungle is concrete. The hunter here is different and so is the hunted. By late afternoon the hunters relax after finishing the day's work. Only then would they turn to look at me and then ask me the same four questions.

Their discussion would then turn towards Tamil Nadu politics. I got a fairly good idea about the welfare schemes announced by the leaders of Tamil Nadu. Every day it was the same boring process. I just wished I was in school. The same boring men and the same boring discussions. But slowly the numbers started to make sense. I learnt about sectors and companies. I understood that these stocks had certain patterns in their movements. It was this *random walk* that these hunters were looking for. CNN business news and NDTV profit were fodder for these men. Terms like share price, Earnings Per Share, market capitalisation and beta stocks started making sense.

After a month of looking at the screen, I wanted to invest. The broker suggested that I invest in Tech Mahindra. He told me the price was down to Rs.556 and would certainly go up to Rs.700. I asked my father for money and opened an account (in my dad's name) and invested in 20 shares. From the very next day, the price of the share started going down by Rs.10 every day. I started getting frustrated. The price finally reached to Rs.460. Now, enough was enough! Never again would I listen to these 'experts' advice.

I had heard about beginner's luck. In my first business venture, I was cheated. In the next venture, I was shown the door and in the third venture, I lost Rs.2000. I got the next shocker. I had no idea about brokerage fees and transaction charges. Another Rs.1000 was deducted from my account.

I then got interested in pharmaceutical stocks. I purchased Glenmark for Rs.855. The very next week, it shot up to Rs.905. This time, I would not take any risk. I sold all the stocks and booked a profit of Rs.2,500. The very next day, the share price of Glenmark shot up to Rs.1,050. I was very depressed for the whole day. Had I waited for one more day, I could have made a profit of Rs.10,000. The world of stocks seemed exciting and unpredictable.

Though I made handsome profits in Cipla, I made losses in BHEL, SBI, TATA Motors and BA Securities. I finally hit the jackpot with Vedanta stocks. I purchased the shares for Rs.74 and sold them for Rs.110 and booked decent profits. In this whole journey of stocks, I have made an overall profit of Rs.4,000 and I gained a lot of experience. One more positive outcome was that I have started reading Business Today and Business Line and they actually make sense. I wish to thank Meenakshi Sundaram uncle for guiding me on how to purchase stocks.

I attended a seminar and a couple of online classes on commodities. I understood terms like Doji candlestick, Fibonacci series, long shadow and bottom shadow, but never ventured into it.

Thanks to this experience, I dream of becoming a great investor. If Warren Buffet believed that he was late at the age of 11 in entering the share market, I think I'm quite late as I am 15. I need to read more books by Warren Buffet in the future.

A quotation by Jim Rohn captivated me. "What is the difference between the poor and the rich? The poor spend the money and save what is left. The rich save the money and spend what is left."

Notes from the parents:

At a Network 21 Seminar, one of the speakers shared a story with us. Somewhere in a school in Europe, a teacher was given two separate classes to teach. One class comprised of students with high I.Q and while the other class consisted of students with mediocre I.Q. At the end of the semester, the teacher was summoned by the school authorities who were surprised to note that the mediocre students had done exceedingly well in their exams and the brilliant students had not performed up to the mark. On interacting with the teacher, they found that the teacher had mistaken the locker number of the students for their I.Q numbers. The mediocre students had locker numbers greater than 140 and the brighter students had locker numbers less than 120.

What the teacher *expected* out of the students was what the students became. We were touched, moved and inspired by this example. The *expectancy* of the parents determines what the child becomes.

Right from Pappu's childhood, we kept looking at her as if she was a genius. Even her frivolous acts were appreciated by us, as the actions of a genius. It was very tough for us as many a time we wanted to give her a piece of our mind. Thanks to the Network 21 speaker, we held our thoughts back.

Even after many years of practising *expectancy*, we develop negative thoughts, but we refrain from sharing these with Pappu.

BUSINESS EXPERIENCES

This was the most interesting aspect of my USY. I had the golden chance of observing different businesses. I spent a period of two weeks at every firm. It was not very easy to get the permission. Many companies refused. Some presumed that I was a secret agent and would share some of the business secrets with their competitors. Some of them were extremely helpful. I wish to give an account of what I learnt at these enterprises.

Ramyas Hotel

It is a well-known hotel located close to the Central Bus Stand in Trichy; even the railway station is nearby. With nearly 100 rooms right from business, executive, deluxe and suite, this hotel has seven halls, right from the conference hall to the marriage hall. It also has a bar, a restaurant and an open air restaurant. There is ample parking space.

I met Mr. Rathnakumar, who is the Proprietor of this hotel. He is a very calm person and a balanced thinker. He introduced me to Ms. Biju. What impressed me were her sparkling eyes and her aquiline nose. She was extremely charming and I felt that she could impress anybody.

She showed me the entire process of housekeeping. This hotel has a software that indicates which room is vacant, which one is occupied and which one has to be cleaned. I sat at the reception for a couple of days and saw how the keys were being handed right from the reception to the housekeeping and back to the reception.

Ramyas Hotel follows the Japanese 5S model. The 5Ss stand for:

Seiri (Sort) – In this hotel, they make room for what you want and remove what is unnecessary. I noticed that there were no unused machines or broken beds. In many hotels I have seen unused material stashed in a corner. Ms. Biju told me that they sold all the unnecessary stuff to create extra space.

Seiso (Set in order) – Ms. Biju stated, "There is a place for everything and everything is in its place". I noted that the marker pen and duster were placed exactly where the label was stuck in the conference hall. In the bathrooms, the soap, towel, shampoo, toothpaste were placed exactly where the labels were pasted. Even in the drawers in the reception desk, there were labels indicating where the notepad should be kept, the number of pens that should be in the stand and the location of the stapler. It was mentioned there should be 20 pens in the stand. I counted and saw, there were exactly 20.

Seiton (Shine) – The entire place was spotless. Every vessel, table, chair and desk was kept spic and span. There was not a speck of dust.

Seiketsu (Standardize) – I noticed a checklist in the laundry indicating what cleaning work had to be done. This had to be ticked or crossed and the items in it were - towels, bed sheets and pillow covers. There were similar checklists in the house keeping department, reception and kitchen.

I have heard people say, that the best way to know about a hotel is to visit the kitchen. The kitchen was well equipped with stoves, rice cookers and microwaves. There were 30 people working there and their head cook was their captain. Everyone's head was covered and they were wearing gloves. I saw non-perishable items like salt, atta, rice and ketchup on one side, while the perishables like fruits and vegetables were kept on the other side. While the non-perishables were purchased once a month, perishables were purchased almost on a daily basis. The team had regular meetings on how much inventory was there and the amount of purchases that needed to be made. For marriages and major functions, the team had to be informed a week in advance for better procurement.

Shitsuke (Sustain) – I was able to observe a meeting where the 5Ss were discussed in detail. Rathnakumar uncle told me that, monthly meetings are conducted on this topic, so that the 5S principles are ingrained in the minds of the people.

Mr. Subroto Bagchi, in his book The High Performance Entrepreneur talks about P/E, 'process to empathy'. I did not understand what it meant while reading the book but I understood it in Hotel Ramyas. The team here not only follows the process, but also practised empathy. I carried my lunch with me on my first day to the hotel. The staff scolded me and told me that I should eat with them till I completed my project. I saw an International Fair being conducted in one of the halls; the staff went and periodically asked their guests what help was required. Whether it was the fixing of banner or helping people with notepad or a glass of water, the team was there at their service. I wanted to see the functioning of the bar. Initially they refused saying that young children were not permitted to go there.

Finally, I was able to spend some time with the bar tenders and observe how they worked.

A.G. Eye Hospital

A.G. Eye Hospital is among the top eye hospitals in India. With the vision of Dr. A. Govindaraj, this hospital was started in the year 1969. Initially, there were only seven beds but now there are 90. Dr. Sherin, a beautiful and elegant lady runs the hospital along with her husband, Dr. Kummararaj. Dr. Sherin is from the Andamans. I was initially made to work at the Reception. The counsellors filled up a card for each patient, which was then handed over to an office assistant. The office assistant would then direct the crowd of patients like a traffic policeman to the requisite doctor.

It was a 'queuing theory' model, which minimised the waiting time of patients. Whether a patient wanted an eye check-up, a power check-up, to purchase a lens or even buy medicines; the whole process was completed quickly. I was the receptionist for a couple of days. I counselled the patients, filled the cards and collected the fees from them.

AG Hospital's counsellors were highly skilled and were empathetic towards the patient's financial challenges. If a patient did not have enough money for the operation, the counsellors would arrange for a bank loan. While talking to children, the counsellors would become childlike. They would change their tone to that of a child and offer them chocolates. The counselors were also very understanding towards the hearing impaired. They spoke to them slowly and wrote down what they said. This procedure helped in better communication with the patients. I understood that this compassion came from Dr. Sherin. Whenever I forgot to wear my spectacles, she would scold me. I realised that if the leader cares for the people, then the team will also do the same.

A very impressive aspect of this hospital was that, the staff rarely took leave. Even if they had to take leave, they would inform well in advance. Also they never moved out of their seat. They were always there to serve the customers. I observed that the only time they left their seats were during the tea and lunch break. The Chief Accountant explained their balance sheets and profit and loss statement to me. She showed me how much they owed the banks and how they went about clearing the loans.

Before completing my project, I was able to interview Dr. Sherin who mentioned that from every case, she learnt something new. Her most challenging case was, saving the eyes of a seven year old boy who fell down from a scooter. She had the boy's picture on her desk. Dr. Sherin works tirelessly. She said that her mission was to give people vision. This gave her energy and drove her to work day in and day out. Aunty also said that she would prepare a to-do list every night. This gave her a clear picture of what work she had to accomplish the next day.

I asked aunty whether she had any other interests. She said that she loved to spend time with her daughters, paint, cook and bake. She would regularly bring cakes for me. They were yummy. I want to do one more project at the hospital.

There is one point that I must mention. My dad lost his spectacles twice during my USY. He just had to make a phone call. From his name and reference number, they would find out his lens power and replace his spectacles. This is the professionalism displayed by the Hospital, in maintaining the records.

Tata Hitachi

We have travelled to Bengaluru by car many times. The entire stretch from Trichy to Karur (76 kilometres) is along the banks of River Cauvery. I would see hundreds of trucks by the river bed and big machines filling the trucks with sand. The entire road till Karur would be full of these trucks. Though the roads are good (there are two tollbooths on the stretch), we could not travel fast as the trucks would leisurely stroll on the road and never make way for us. I would complain to my parents about the casual behaviour of the truck drivers. It was only later, that I was told, that it is one of the biggest businesses in Tamil Nadu. These trucks of sand feed the construction industry. I had also seen the big machines at the granite quarries near Madurai but had never given it a second thought.

It was only when I went for my training to Tata Hitachi that everything fell in place.

At the Dealer's office I found only three people: a person looking after administration, one looking after spare parts and an office boy. I wondered what kind of a business this was.

What I saw was an eye opener. The dealers Mr. Manohar & Mrs. Subashini Manohar dealt with two models - EX120 (the bucket of this loader could lift 12 tonnes of weight) and EX220 (the bucket of this loader would lift 22 tonnes of weight). So, how were they sold? Ms. Jayanthi the person in charge, said that they follow the three Ss... Sales, Service and Spares. So whom did they sell these machines to? She said that they were sold to mine owners, quarry owners and river sand sellers. How did they buy it? Mr. Manohar, the Director, explained the entire purchasing process. He said that each machine cost 50 - 60 lakhs. As the money involved was huge, some of the buyers preferred to hire the machine while others preferred to own it. Uncle explained that the sales team not only generated enquiries and brought orders but also arranged for finance. Kotak Mahindra was the financier for this purchase. Now I knew what Kotak Mahindra was doing and how they made the money.

The selling process was very interesting. The team would regularly go through the newspapers to find out what tenders were being released in the construction business. They knew that a tender meant that some customer would have to purchase their equipment. They would also scout around their entire territory to find out where a new mine or quarry was opening. Mr. Manohar mentioned that the lifespan of a machine is three to four years maximum. Therefore the sales person would reach the customer's spot just before the machine was about to breathe its last. They could then replace the old machine with the new. Wow! That is some business.

They also had a team of Engineers and Technicians who would rush to the spot, when a machine broke down. They call that Service. To support the Service department they had a Spares department. Again, I came across the word, inventory control. At Ramyas Hotel, they talked about the inventory control of food items. At A. G. Hospital, they talked about the inventory control of lenses and medicines and at Tata Hitachi, they talked about the inventory control of spares. The items which they stocked were essential and were less in value. The high value items were procured from the head office.

Karur Vysya Bank

Can you guess what is advertised the most in my town? It is not dresses, it is not jewellery, it is not even hotels or shops; it is coaching for bank exams. There are giant hoardings of bank exam institutes. The newspapers are replete with banking exam coaching advertisements. The bus panels talk about bank exam institutes. I thought that banking must be the best job in the world. Many students whom I met have the dream of getting a job in a bank. My next project took me all the way to Madurai. I was all set to get trained in Karur Vysya Bank.

I was introduced to Mr. Natarajan, a banker. He had a cheerful face, wore thick rimmed spectacles and had sparkling eyes. Natarajan uncle was a great teacher and communicator. He gave very good analogies that even a layman like me could understood.

Here, I had a hands on experience. Uncle asked me to open an account. I had to meticulously go through a lot of details while filling up the form.

Terms like KYC, Current Account and Savings Account were painstakingly explained to me by Uncle. He said that Current Account is used for business dealing and multiple transactions can be done in a day. He said Savings Account can be used by one to a maximum of four joint holders but only one transaction can be done in a day.

Later, Natarajan uncle gave me a few challans. There was a DD challan, cheque, cheque slip and deposit slip. He taught me how to fill all the challans. He also explained the rules to follow while filling the challans.

I gathered that every Account Number had meaning. The first two numbers indicated the bank where the account was held. The next four numbers depended on the branch. The next seven digits displayed the personal account number. The last two digits denoted the product that was being used (current account, savings account etc.)

The bank had two data entry operators, a few Cashiers, a person to assist in filling the challans and opening accounts, a person for giving loan against gold and a gold appraiser. There was also a pot bellied security guard who roamed around aimlessly. He must have been sure that no robber would come and attack this branch. There was also a locker room and cameras all around.

The staff reported directly to the Manager, who had to shoulder a lot of responsibilities. A customer walked in to encash a cheque worth Rs. 4,00,000. The manager called the account holder to verify whether the person with the cheque was genuine or not.

Once there was a hilarious incident. A client had come to the bank to repay a loan. This client could not remit the entire amount. He requested the manager to 'adjust'. The manager was livid. The client did not seem to realise that the bank is a professional organisation and not a place to 'adjust'. The manager was friendly and in spite of all his work stress explained to me how a loan could be availed. He said that a loan should be given only if the money would be put to productive use. The borrower needed to have the right credentials and sufficient collateral to repay the loans.

Now I know why students, including engineers want to work in a bank. They probably think that this job is easy. They think that they can lead comfortable lives, earn a good monthly salary, grow big bellies and retire. The term used in our town for this is 'settle'. But I feel that the industry should be run by professionals who are truly passionate about banking. I am now aware that banking is to India what blood is to my body.

Vagus Technologies (BPO)

I have heard about Chetan Bhagat's book, 'One Night at the Call Centre'. I always thought that call centres and BPOs were a place where people sit and make calls at night. They talk in another accent and attend to customer complaints. When I went to Nehru Memorial College, I saw a Medical Transcription unit. Finally, my training at Vagus helped me see the larger picture.

Vagus is a RPO (Recruitment Process Outsourcing) and works for e- Biz, a company in the USA. e-Biz has many customers in the US. These customers need Java developers, Oracle programmers and Microsoft technologists. e-Biz would outsource the orders to Vagus technologies. The recruitment team of Vagus Technologies would then go to job portals like USMonster.com and Naukri.com. For example, if Wipro needed a java expert in the USA, they would contact e-biz, which would outsource their order to Vagus and Vagus would search and find a suitable candidate. The Vagus marketing team would then convince the candidate to relocate.

The candidate would sign the contract with Wipro but be on the pay rolls of E-Biz. When the contract expires, E-Biz would try to place the candidate in another company. The H1B visa terms would have to be changed for this and Vagus had a visa transfer team.

The teams would work in the nights to match US timings. They had a dress code and worked from Monday to Friday. If they failed to meet their targets, they had to work on Saturday as well.

Initially, some of the employees pulled my leg for wasting time instead of studying in school. But later, they became very good friends of mine. Ms. Shanmuga Priya, one of the employees was extremely supportive and friendly and drilled the business process into my head. But for Ms. Priya, I would have never understood what was happening at Vagus.

Naturals

I had gone to Naturals many times for hairdressing. But this time my aim was different. I had to study their business. Every day, I would see a number of people, mostly women, coming here with a wish to enhance their beauty. On auspicious days, the numbers would swell. The members of the staff work from 9 in the morning to 9 in the evening. I observed that an average of twenty customers walked in everyday. Each customer was charged Rs.1000 to Rs.2000 for the service. I made a mental calculation that the turnover would be at least Rs.30,000 per day. The things that captivated me about this place were the name, the logo design and their brand ambassadors Kareena Kapoor & Genelia.

The next alluring aspect about Naturals was their interiors. The mauve walls, fragrance, glass partition, aesthetically designed seating area, beautiful layout and wonderful display of cosmetics were mesmerizing. There was not a speck of dust on the floor.

The next part I like about Naturals was the staff. I was surprised to see that most of the people working there were from North-East

India. I tried to find out why. The answer... they were fair and good looking, they could smile and talk in a friendly tone with the customer, they knew how to dress well, they spoke good English and most importantly they were willing to relocate to any location. The North Easterners were given a place to live and provided with proper amenities. I later gathered that this professional team was trained at the corporate office in Chennai, which maintained a database of all its trainees. Whenever there was a requirement, these people would be deployed to the place where the franchisee required support.

The customers were given membership cards and offered generous discounts. This ensured that Naturals got repeat customers.

I could comprehend the franchise model. A business idea which proved successful in one location could be replicated in as many locations as possible. I was able to connect this concept with Mr. Subroto Bagchi's term "Fractals". I could also connect the scalability of Mindtree with that of Naturals. Naturals and its franchises are one good family. The franchises had to invest nearly 50 lakhs and Naturals would provide the idea, the design and the logistics. The logistics included staff and cosmetics. Thanks to my friend Naren in Singapore, I could perceive how the logistics worked.

Naturals is the brainchild of Mr & Mrs. C. K. Kumaravel. Mr. Kumaravel initially launched a brand called Raga Herbal Powder, which was a success. He then introduced Raga Soap, Raga Hair oil and Raga Paste, which failed. He then got into a litigation and had to close the company. It immediately struck me that Mr. C. K. Kumaravel could have made the mistake of going for line extension, as I had read in the book "Positioning". But, Kumaravel uncle was a fighter. He and his wife learnt from Anita Roddick of Body Shop, how the beauty business worked. Now, there was no turning back. They made a model suitable to the Indian environment. Today, they have 450+ franchises in their network. I have heard one of his quote which goes "Look at the sun and you cannot see the shadows."

I wish to thank Vanaja Shanmugasundram aunty because of whom I gained memorable experience.

Time Kids

When I was six years old, I had gone on a holiday to Singapore with my parents. One day, I was travelling by bus with them. My parents were sitting in a different seat and I was next to an uncle. As the bus moved, I kept reading the signboards on the shops loudly. The uncle turned to me and asked me my age. When I said I was six, he was surprised. He told me that children in Singapore went to school only after the age of seven. It was only later that, that they learnt to read and write.

Time Kids is a well known pre-school in Trichy. They lay the foundation for a successful school life. I could sense a big business opportunity over here. Given the size of our population and the eagerness of the parents to give an early start to their children, pre-school in India is the necessity. I loved the kids of Time Kids. They were cute darlings. Initially, they did not talk to me. Once they understood that I was in the same category as them, they became my best friends. This was the place where I did not go as a business observer. I would have fun with the children the whole day.

The pre KG children were being trained about colours. They had a colour of the week and knew how to associate colours with various objects. The syllabus of the LKG and UKG kids was astonishingly of a very high standard. The kids had to learn addition, multiplication, tough words and their usage. I never knew this till my third standard. There was also a separate class for mentally challenged children.

The Time Kids franchisee was also running a yoga business and a Hindi tuition centre. Thanks to Priya Vanraj aunty for providing me with this wonderful opportunity.

Gramalaya – An NGO

An innocuous looking office with a name board that was not visible, but the kind of work they do there, can jolt anyone out of their wits. Gramalaya is the creation of Mr. Dhamodharan. It is a thirty year old organisation that has expertise in the field of rural development. Our Prime Minister Modiji has the vision of building 10 crore smart toilets in India. 1 crore of these are going to be built by Gramalaya in South India.

I went for a field visit to their training centre which was 45 kilometres from Trichy. There were 15 other trainees from interior Karnataka. The entire training program took place in Kannada and it was very difficult for me to comprehend. They then took us around the place which was very colourful. With painted walls, it almost looked like a park.

We learnt about septic tank, leach pit and compost pit. Each system has its own advantages when it comes to treating waste. They demonstrated how we could construct bio-toilets both Indian and western. They showed us smart toilets where tissue paper is used. The paper is later burnt in an incinerator. I was concerned that this could cause pollution.

They explained their business model to me. Gramalaya's marketing team would scout for villages which did not have toilets. They would convince the villagers and invite them for a workshop. The villagers would be provided boarding and lodging during their training. They would then be assisted in building toilets in their village. For these projects, Gramalaya obtained loans from the banks. On completion of the project, the report would be submitted to the Government which would then reimburse the expenses.

I have a humble suggestion. The Government should insist that a dozen trees are planted around every toilet. That way 10 crore toilets would lead to the planting of 120 crore trees.

These business experiences took me from hotel management, to hospital management, from how dealerships work, to the working of banks. I also learnt about the functioning of BPOs, how franchise model works and finally, how NGOs serve the country. I am extremely grateful to all the people who helped me and supported me in this endeavour.

Notes from the parents:

We were addressing a few engineering graduates. We asked them to share their dreams. They unanimously said that getting a job which paid them Rs.10,000/- would be enough. If they had to aspire for such a meager salary after four years of engineering, why did they have to do engineering at all? Rs.10,000/- per month would amount to Rs.400/- per day. This amount could be earned by going door to door and selling soaps and detergents.

In our family, money was an evil word. When we were young, we never dreamt that we could generate wealth on our own. As our parents were employees, we were programmed and mentally conditioned to depend upon an employer, who would take care of our lives.

We did not want Sagarikka to have the same mindset. Her network marketing experience gave her the confidence that she could be *financially independent*. We gave her Rs.20,000/- to invest in the stock market. Initially, she developed cold feet. Fear of failure was holding her back. Though we were willing to partake in the investment, Sagarikka had to overcome a lot of inner resistance to gain momentum and enter the world of stocks. It dawned on us that she may have never done it in the later stages of her life, as society would condition her into a job mindset.

If Mark Zuckerberg, Tim Sykes, Micheal Dell or Steve Job could make it big by their early 20's. Why can't we Indians?

If only the youth of India could enter the world of business and stocks, early in life, could that create a million start ups? Could that eliminate the craze for Government jobs? Could that solve the unemployment problem in the country?

TRAVELOGUES

WANDERING FEET

WANDERING FEET

The most exciting part of my USY was my travel. Two of my expeditions were to Mount Kailash and Leh, while another one took me to the heart of Cuddalore. Let me unravel what happened.

Mount Kailash

It was my mother's dream to visit Mount Kailash, which is known as the home of Lord Shiva. The confirmation of the travel was as big an adventure as the journey itself. We had planned the trip with the Isha Group and booking was the easy part. Then, an earthquake, 7.3 on the Richter Scale struck Nepal. The country was devastated and the aftershocks could be felt a thousand kilometres away.

The usual route to Mount Kailash is via Lhasa, Tibet, which is under the control of China. Due to the earthquake, the regular route got blocked. It was up to the Chinese to open up a new route for us to get darshan of Lord Shiva.

Every day was like the final over of a one day match. My parents kept pestering the Isha authorities and asking them when we would get the permit to Mount Kailash. What could the poor authorities do? It was for the Chinese to decide.

Meanwhile, we had already purchased the necessary equipment for the journey. Purchasing the apparel itself was an adventure. We had to hunt all over Chennai for the necessary clothing. One shop had jackets, while another had shoes and the third one had socks. The cost of these was exorbitant; and we were not sure whether the programme was on or not. I wanted to say, Oh Chinese, Have mercy on us!

And finally, it happened. The permit came and we were destined to go to Mount Kailash.

We landed in Kathmandu on September 15, 2015. Forty-five of us were packed into a bus and taken to Hotel Shangrila. None of us smiled at each other during the journey, perhaps because we were all tired and also because our culture prevents us from smiling at strangers. We had a training programme in the evening, where mainly videos of Sadhguru were shown and words of advice were given by our team leaders.

Sadhguru stated that just as pressure increases as we go deep into the sea, pressure decreases as we climb the mountains. He said that jumping around and other such antics could prove dangerous and may even be fatal. I got scared as I had not come so far to die. We were then asked to take precautions by drinking three litres of water every day, do certain exercises and pack minimal luggage. Medical test was compulsory twice a day. It then struck me… This was not a holiday, it was an expedition. Coming back alive was my goal.

We went sightseeing the next day. It was the day of the Dashain festival. Wherever we went, the Durbar Square, the Vishnu Temple or Thamel, there were beautiful women everywhere. They were all dressed in red sarees, had huge bindis and were adorned with flowers. They kept smiling all the time and I kept taking selfies with them whenever possible.

Most of the buildings had been destroyed by the earthquake. Some temples had even been razed to the ground. My guide told me that he was lucky to be alive and shared stories about people who had lost their livelihood.

We then went to see the living goddess, Kumari Devi. She lives in Kumari Ghar, a palace in the centre of the city. She is believed to be the incarnation of Goddess Durga. We were taken into the room in which the goddess lives. She is never allowed to come out of the palace. Once a year, she is taken around the city so that people can get a glimpse of her. When I met her face to face I was horrified. She was a young girl of about eight years old. She was seated on a throne and decked up in jewels and bright clothes. I thought she looked very sad as she gave me the prasad. I think she would have preferred to come out and play with me on the streets instead of carrying the burden of the world on her tiny shoulders.

Our next destination was Nepal Gunj. Surprisingly, it is only three kilometres away from Uttar Pradesh, India. It is a small town with a small airport. Later, a team of cooks and helpers also joined us from there for the rest of our journey.

We then took off to Simikot. I was alloted a seat in a chartered seven seater flight. I was sitting just behind the pilot and observed every manoeuvre of his. We landed in a beautiful hamlet in the midst of the mountains called Simikot. Cold air hit my face as soon as I stepped out of the plane. We had to walk to a hotel on the hilltop. The altitude made a big difference. It was no longer like trudging on the roads of Chennai. Every step was getting more difficult. We were nestled in a small hotel on the mountain top. Here my journey of discomfort began. The toilets and rooms had to be shared. The night was freezing cold. The food consisted of mainly chappati and dal. Every meal had potatoes. There were potatoes for breakfast, potatoes for lunch and potatoes for dinner.

The next day, we had to go on an eight kilometre trek to acclimatize ourselves to the climatic conditions. It wasn't all that easy as oxygen here is rarefied. The vegetation is sparse and mainly ragi is grown here. Patches of pumpkin, cabbage and apple trees are all around the place. We went to a Lord Shiva temple and saw the Karnali River flowing down below. The temple was bristling with children all around. They mobbed us and begged us for food. The children here were extremely dirty and unkempt. I kept taking photographs of them and showed them the pictures. They were bewildered. They had no access to education and mainly resorted to begging for food from the tourists.

I noticed that the men here gossip and while away their time, while women do all the manual work like digging ditches, farming, repair work, selling and also taking care of the children. My dad and some of the other male co-travellers were highly enthused seeing this. They wished that the Indian women could adopt this culture, so that the Indian men could lead happier lives!

We had to leave by chopper the next morning. The team leader decided that the elderly people and especially who were heavy should leave by the first chopper. The logic was that agile, younger ones could take the last chopper. As there were only three stout, elderly people in our team, there was room for one more person of lesser weight. Our team leader requested a girl senior to me by age to accompany those elderly people. The girl refused stating that she wanted to go with her family. That was when I volunteered. I was the youngest in the group and the people applauded me for my courage. By this action, I was able to win the hearts of people and became the darling of the team.

The next morning we took off to Hilsa. While Simikot is at 9,500 feet above sea level, Hilsa is 14,000 feet above sea level. Flying by helicopter is the only way to reach Hilsa. The chopper ride was the ride of a lifetime. The pilot had to cross a series of mountains to reach Hilsa. I could feel the power of the mountains from close. Each peak was strong, majestic and magnificent. The pilot would swerve between the peaks and then we would confront another peak. Often, I would feel that the pilot would dash against the awe-inspiring mountain, but then we would take off vertically in the nick of time and go to the next mountain top. I felt, I could almost touch it with my hands. It was that close. The thirty minute chopper ride was the most exciting and scariest ride of my life. Though I am not a religious person, I started chanting Ganesha, Hanuman and Durga slokas. Finally, the helicopter emerged out of the mountains and we saw a plain strip of land. Humans at last! The landing was even more frightening. The pilot took a 180 degree turn and landed the chopper. Whew!

Hilsa is a small strip of land. It was extremely windy here. It was freezing. We had warm soup and chapatis and waited for the entire team to arrive at Hilsa. We then had to cross a long suspension bridge over the Karnali River into China. The bridge kept swaying from side to side. We were told not to look down as the sight might frighten us. Naughty as I was (as I am), I kept looking down. It was great fun.

We crossed the bridge and reached China (Tibet). We were made to wait for more than an hour. As there were many cameras all around, the entire team requested me not to misbehave. Mr. Ramesh (a salt factory owner from Tuticorin), Karthik (an Architect from Chennai), Mr. Aravind (who never told me what he did) and Dr. Kavitha (Paediatrist from Bengaluru) were my companions. We would constantly crack jokes and take a dig at one another.

Finally, the Chinese buses came. A soldier checked our passports as we entered our buses. He checked my photo twice, then thrice. I made an expression so that I could resemble my passport photo as closely as possible. Then we went to another check post. We were asked to get down from our buses and our baggage was inspected not once but twice. They scrutinised our faces too. A young Chinese soldier looked at my passport and gave me a cold stare. I gave him a very innocent look, lest he suspect me to be a RAW agent.

We were dumped into a bus that looked like a Volvo. Here everything was Chinese. There were no imported product. Buses, cars and bikes were all made in China. We were taken to a town 14,000 feet above sea level called Taklakot, to the supposedly most posh hotel there called "The Purang Hotel". Our baggage was once again checked. I was carrying a book on Sathyajit Ray. The officials opened the book, read parts of it and even closely observed the photos in it. I was amazed that the Chinese took such a deep interest in Sathyajit Ray. It was only later that I was told that they were looking for any literature or photos that spread the message of Free Tibet and Dalai Lama. This was China occupied Tibet. "Imagine me being an agent of Dalai Lama!"

Every building in Taklakot had a Chinese flag. There were cameras all over the town. Every product right from soft drinks to mineral water, chips, shoes and chocolates were all of Chinese make. The TV programmes were all in Chinese. There was no BBC or any English channel. The programs had no advertisements. I came to know that even Google and Facebook do not operate in China, as the Chinese have their own version of them.

We walked around the streets after a medical check up to tune ourselves to the oxygen levels. We trekked to the cave of a Buddhist prince who had 2500 wives but could not find happiness. He married yet again for the 2501st time, when he found true happiness. The 2500 wives were jealous of the 2501st wife. So the prince hid her in a cave. The men (my co- travellers) were delighted to hear this story. They tried to make their wives understand that their happiness lies in going beyond one wife. There is one aspect of Chinese culture that I admired. Devotees stashed cash in the walls of this cave as a form of prayer. Though there was a lot of money strewn around, not a penny was touched. I imagined what would happen if one tried to do the same thing in India. That is what character is. Kudos to the Chinese!

All hell broke loose at Taklakot that night. The hotel had no amenities. The faucets were leaking. Hot water was not available. There was no room service. There was no receptionist in the hotel. Picture out a hotel with no reception desk, no room service and no restaurant. It was like a ghost hotel.

The next horror! The doctors started their regular check. The blood pressure of my fellow travellers was shooting up. My mother's blood pressure was 250. Some of them started getting splitting headaches while the others had a blurred vision. I also joined the bandwagon. I started vomiting and felt dehydrated. The doctors were on a war footing. The chief, Dr. Anbu was like a man possessed. He scolded some of the patients for not taking medicines properly. Medicines were being administered left, right and centre. Diamox (medicine for higher altitudes) was a must. The oxygen levels and pulse rate of certain people were coming down. Dr. Anbu was on a mission and was ably assisted by Dr. Kavitha and Dr. Sivaram. They had to take this group to Mount Kailash and bring them back safely.

One couple in particular was funny. They did not bring warm clothing. They even refused to take tablets. The husband had high blood sugar, blood pressure and numerous other ailments. His wife did not want to be left behind; she also had many physical complaints. Then why were they not taking proper medications? They believed that if they were the true devotees of Shiva, the lord would take care of them. Could religion cloud our common sense?

Next morning we took off in a bus to Manasarovar. En route we stopped at Rakshas Tal. It's a huge lake with crystal clear water. I was not allowed to go near the lake as according to folklore, this lake is possessed by evil spirits. It is also known as Ravana Tal. Rakshas Ravana did severe penance here. The water here is salty and it is surprising, because, the water in Lake Manasarover, 2 kilometres away, is fresh. There is no aquatic life in this lake as it is poisonous. I tried to Google search on how two huge lakes, very close to each other could have different characteristics? I found no answer.

Manasarovar is an ethereal lake. We rested in a guest house, which had been built by the Parmathinikethan group from Rishikesh. I was standing in line for my regular check-up and drinking hot soup. Someone rushed into the room and whispered something into Dr. Anbu's ears. Immediately, he and a couple of others dashed out of the room knocking me over in the process. My soup was spilled all over. Something terrible must have happened. Where was dad by the way? He was missing. Mom and I rushed to the emergency room and found the doctors attending to my dad. He was being given oxygen. He had been afflicted with AMS (Acute Mountain Sickness), which makes a person disoriented. A person with AMS walks around like he is drunk and people's voices sound weird to him as though they are coming from a cave.

Fortunately, dad was alert enough to inform somebody and was saved. Otherwise, he would have had to cancel the trip and rush down to lesser altitude. Whew!

For the first time in my life I had to use open toilets. I was cautioned not to go alone. There were man-eating dogs all around, which were as big as wolves.

The next morning, Dr. Sivaram and a group of others stated that they had seen some super natural and bizarre occurrences at Manasarovar Lake the previous night. They said that they saw the saptarishis descend from the heavens and take a dip in the lake. I decided that I had to see this the next night. I woke up the next morning at the Bramhamuhurtha (4.30 am) and went near the lake. The heavens were remarkable. The stars seemed strange. One star in particular seemed freakish and looked as though it was about to touch the lake. Sadly, I never saw the saptarishis. The gods must have been angry with me!

The previous afternoon, we performed rituals at the lake. We then took a dip in the freezing waters which was refreshing. I saw stones stacked all around in different conical patterns. Dad told me that some Shamam rituals must have taken place here. Then a very unfortunate incident occurred. Bala uncle, one of the friendliest and cutest persons in our group developed severe breathing difficulty. His oxygen levels were precariously down to 65 percent. Dr. Anbu instructed that Bala uncle should be rushed to Taklakot Hospital. He could not make it to Mount Kailash.

The next day, we trekked to Mount Kailash from 16,000 feet to 17,500 feet. My parents took a pony ride. My trek was a lovely experience. The air was fresh and the atmosphere silent. A rivulet kept us company till the very end. At one place, there were a few nomadic tents which sold hot noodles, water and tea. Food had never been tastier.

Talking about food, our team of cooks was headed by Mr. Thangka. He was also our tour guide and was responsible for organising our journey from Kathmandu to Mount Kailash and back. These cooks would serve us hot tea and biscuits, bread, boiled vegetables, soup, sweet kheer and fresh, neatly cut fruits. They even treated us to some popcorn. I was woken up every morning and treated to hot tea or soup. The cooks fondly called me gudiya and took a liking to me. They would always smile and whenever I asked for any help, they happily obliged. I wondered how people in the harshest of conditions are always happy and people down in the plains in the most pleasant of conditions are sad, irritated or depressed?

The day after reaching Mount Kailash, we went on an outer parikrama. The swamiji asked us to imagine Lord Shiva to be a child and call out to him gently. A few devotees got hysterical and started wailing and crying. The whole air was filled with sobs, shouts and screams. I was worried that baby Shiva would run away on seeing the agony of his devotees. Mount Kailash was really, really beautiful. I sat on a rock and kept admiring its grandeur. I soaked in the atmosphere and spent the rest of the day looking at the mountain as I chatted with various groups of people.

I reached Taklakot the next morning ahead of most of the others. I waited for my parents to arrive. Finally, when they came, my mother was being carried by a few people. She was writhing in pain. While coming down the mountains, her horse had gone wild. It started jumping up and down due to which she had lost her balance. One leg of hers had been hooked to the saddle and she was dragged by the horse. The horse kept going in circles and mom kept screaming all the time. The horse keepers finally got hold of the animal, but enough damage had been done. X-rays later revealed that she had three dislocations and three hairline fractures.

The Isha Group is the most professional group I have ever seen. At every station, right from Kathmandu to Simikot, a coordinator was present to receive us and take care of us. At every leg of the journey, we were told what to do and what not to do, how to behave, the importance of drugs and how to interact with the Chinese officials. Taking 45 people all the way up to Mount Kailash and bringing them back in one piece is not a joke. Hats off to the Isha Group.

Finally, I was back in Chennai, in one atmospheric pressure and enjoying hot idlis, sambar and chutney… but my heart longs to go back to the solitude and the mystique of the mountains.

Leh, Ladakh

My parents could not accompany me on this trip which was planned by the Ramanans from Trichy. This passionate nature loving couple has been travelling to the mountains for the last 35 years.

There were ten of us in the group. Mr. Rahul from Delhi was the trip organiser and team leader. Mr. Norboo was our guide. There were also a few cooks and helpers. After acclimatising ourselves for a day, we went to Thiksey Monastery. There is a huge statue of Maitreya (future Buddha), which is forty feet in height and covers almost two floors of the monastery. I learnt that Maitreya would appear on Earth when we attain complete enlightenment and teach us dharma.

The main objective of this trip was to observe and study some of the tribes and villages situated around this area. It was a unique experience for all of us to stay with the villagers for nearly four to five days. We had the fabulous experience of watching their day - to - day life from very close quarters. We learnt about their culture, food, dressing, music and how they earn their livelihood etc. I had the opportunity of visiting five villages out of which I found two very fascinating. Garkhon and Darchik, huddled in the lower territory of Dah Hanu Valley. Drokpas and Brogpas are the Red Aryans living here. There is a theory that says that these people are the descendants of Alexander the Great. The traditional music of Ladakh includes the instruments like surna and daman (shehnai and drum). Tibetian music is an integral part of the religion. It involves complex religious chanting. Religious mask dances are also an important part of Ladakh's cultural life. All the major Ladakhi monasteries hold an annual mask dance festival. The typical costumes of the locals include Gonchas of velvet (head cover), boots, hats and elaborately embroidered waistcoats.

Their main source of income is agriculture. During summers, they grow large quantities of apricots, apples, grapes and store it for later use in winter. Their staple food is tsampa and namkin chai. Tsampa is a useful trekking food as it can be consumed without cooking. Frankly speaking, I could not savour the taste of thukpa (noodle soup) and tsampa (roasted barley flour). It was unpalatable!

The most exciting part of our trip was the wildlife trekking. Ladakh is famous for its rich wildlife. The animals which we spotted were wild yak, Asiatic ibex, Ladakh urial, red fox, Tibetian wolf and snow leopard. The population of the snow leopards is dwindling. Currently, there are only 50 of them in the Ladakh Valley. We spotted three snow leopards. They had a very dignified appearance. We spotted many birds like the black redstart, common rosefinch, black – billed magpie, golden eagle and lammergeier. The start of any trek is usually boring and this was no different. We would walk for a long time and sight nothing. The moment we spotted a bird or an animal, our tiredness would instantly vanish. Our energy levels would reach the peak and we would be back on our job. We would do what decent Homo sapiens on the planet should do, click photos and look at our finds through the binoculars.

Every aspect of the trip was exciting and thrilling, be it the food or attending to nature's call. The food was planned, packed and given to us. The packet usually consisted of a boiled egg, boiled potato, omelette stuffed inside chapatti or poori and cream biscuits. If you notice, most of them are energy providers. The toilets were even more intriguing and known as chaksa. It is a small room with a small hole dug in the middle. The waste is collected and later used as fuel and fertilizer.

Something mysterious happened in a place, 30 kilometres away from Leh. It is called the Magnetic Hill. Here, the land creates an optical illusion. Though it slopes downhill, it appears to be uphill. The engine of our van was switched off. What happened next was an astounding experience. The car appeared to be moving up the hill though it was supposed to be going down. I still have not been able to understand this phenomenon.

We used to spend our nights sitting around the bhukhari. We had to constantly fuel it with wood to keep ourselves warm. Then it was story time. The Ramanans kept us engaged by telling us about how the idol of Srirangam had been rescued from the Nizam. Currently they are working on a book based on this story. Rahul uncle would terrorise us with ghost stories and I used to be frightened to go to the toilet in the night. I could see ghosts and phantoms coming out of the chaksa. I also had a spooky experience. I was out in the dark and could see my friend Hetal come at a distance. She kept coming closer. I was appalled when I saw her standing next to me. Then I turned to see the Hetal who was at a distance. She had vanished into thin air. I was petrified and I wondered why I hadn't experienced such a phenomenon in the city?

After coming back to Leh, I met a Ladakhi who was instrumental in saving India. He was up in the mountains when he spotted a few Pakistani soldiers infiltrating into the country and immediately informed the Indian Army. That was the start of the Kargil War. I took selfies with this hero.

Providence was testing me. I was put in a separate flight to Delhi. Why does the youngest one always have to suffer? My other team members would come by the next flight an hour later. At the Delhi airport, I misplaced my cell phone. I started to panic and ran all over the airport.

That was when I saw the famous cricketer, Gautham Gambhir. He smiled at me and I started to cry. Two reasons. One, I could not find my cellphone and two, I missed a golden opportunity to take a selfie with Gambhir. Thankfully, I found the phone at the help desk later but I would not be able to show my friends the photo that I could have taken with Gambhir.

At the Chennai airport, I could not find my boarding pass. The airport authorities did not permit me to leave the airport. This was too much stress in one day and I started to cry again. I thought that I would have to stay at the airport for the rest of my life. Ms. Fathima Bathool Maluk (MASTeR college proprietrix) came to my rescue. Aunty convinced the airport authorities that I was a girl from a respectable family and not a terrorist as they may have thought.

If silence is a tangible commodity, Ladakh would have been its largest exporter. The people here have also mastered the art of smiling. I wish the Ladakhis could export their silence and smile to the cities.

Cuddalore

December, 2015 was one of the worst months in the history of Chennai. A city known for its water scarcity, turned into a lake. It became the Venice of India! Boats became the only mode of transport and this incident brought out the character of the Chennaites. Students, families, actors and artistes forgot the differences between them and went all out to save the city.

But, there is one place which was even worse hit; Cuddalore. It did not get as much media attention as Chennai. The whole town of Cuddalore was marooned for a few days and there were more deaths reported over there.

One of my parents' student from TRICHY PLUS, Mr. Dharaneedar from Oxford Engg. College, took the first initiative. He organised a bus with the support of Saranathan College to Cuddalore. I was moved by what happened next. The students came from all quarters and a bus load of supplies was sent to Cuddalore. Unfortunately, some political groups prevented the bus from entering Cuddalore and the bus was diverted to Chennai.

Now my mother stepped in. She set out on a mission to help the people of Cuddalore. Fathima Bathool aunty extended her support to this cause.

She organised the college bus and sent her students with some supplies. Many other good Samaritans extended a helping hand and my mom was able to organise a bus full of supplies.

I wish to share one particular incident. Ms. Naveena (a staff member of Trichy Plus) has been supporting an old man and giving him Rs.1200 a month for quite some time now. That month, the old man refused to accept the amount and asked her to donate it to the people of Cuddalore instead. He said, they needed it even more. This poor man even purchased blankets worth Rs. 600 from his meagre savings and asked Naveena to donate it. I know that many celebrities and philanthropists had donated their savings but this act of the old man was the kindest of them all.

We collected a bus load of clothes, plantains, water, biscuits, notebooks, sachets of cooking oil, medicines, blankets and toiletries.

We (the team from TRICHY PLUS and MASTeR College) started our journey at 6 am. At the outskirts of Cuddalore, near Panruti, there was a rehabilitation centre. Here, the volunteers and police were extremely supportive. They informed us of the localities where help had already reached. We were also informed of places where help was required. We were accompanied by a constable on our journey.

The first village we entered was Vairakuppam. We distributed our supplies to 60 families. We saw a community kitchen, which feeds 10,000 people. In spite of such a calamity, the people asked us to join them for the community lunch. We gracefully declined.

Our next stop was a remote village in the deep interiors of Cuddalore. Our bus driver was fuming and fretting as the roads were unsafe. The fields were inundated and there were huge tracts of water everywhere.

Finally, we reached Therukupallineerodai. There were 120 families living there whose houses had been destroyed and they had no food. What touched me was that these people were very calm, in spite of such a traumatic experience. They stood patiently in a line as we distributed the provisions. What happened next was even more touching. These villagers climbed coconut trees and brought down coconuts and offered us tender coconut water.

Something very upsetting happened next. A group of 50 families waited nearby, and did not want to join this group. Since they belonged to the upper caste, they refused to accept supplies along with the other group, supposedly the Dalits. I saw the true colours of India here. The roots of casteism are entrenched deep within our society.

We then stopped at a school. The children were thrilled and squealed with joy when we delivered the supplies. By now it was late evening and none of us had had breakfast or lunch. We had a delicious dinner late in the evening. One thing is for sure, there is no shortage of help in this country. The only thing we require is to dissolve our differences and come together.

Notes from the parents:

You may recall the lecture given by *Virus* in '3 Idiots'. Life begins as a race, where the first of the million sperms to hit the ovum, wins and manifests into a being.

Competing for clearing the IITs, AIIMS or the IAS entrance exams is all a race. Charles Darwin's 'survival of the fittest' concept runs all across the society. We had a choice – we could either make *Pappu run in the race or create her own space.* We were influenced by the thought provoking book 'Positioning' by Al Ries & Jack Trout. The authors mention that the real winner is the one who is the first to enter the minds of the people in a particular category.

We come across numerous examples - for instance how Aravind Kejriwal was able to position himself in the minds of the public. R.K Narayan created his own space as well. Dr.APJ Abdul Kalam, the missile man of India, was able to carve a niche for himself. So have Vishwanathan Anand, Amitabh Bachchan, Baba Ramdev, Arunima Sinha, Usha Uthup, Ritish Agarwal, Arnab Goswami and many others.

We kept on driving this point in Pappu's mind and let her explore and unearth a space for herself.

Finally the choice is hers – whether to compete or complete....

One quote still lingers in our mind – the trouble with being in the rat race is that, even if you win, you are still a rat.

VARIETY - THE SPICE OF LIFE

- VISIT TO THE 'MAKE IN INDIA' INDUSTRIES
- THE KALEIDOSCOPIC EXPERIENCES

VISIT TO THE 'MAKE IN INDIA' INDUSTRIES

SRF

We travel thousands of kilometres by car. I have always wondered 'How does the tyre take such an enormous load?' Indian roads are usually not predictable and famous for their potholes. The tyre takes a beating and still keeps moving. I uncovered the secret at SRF Industries. SRF has plants in Chennai, Gurgaon, South Africa, Thailand, UAE and Trichy.

The factory resembled a five star hotel. I was expecting to see the manufacturing process. Instead, the whole discussion riveted around Human Resources. Mr. Krishnan, the HR Head was passionate about discussing employee welfare. Employees would be treated to birthday gifts, wedding gifts, Diwali celebration, summer camps, medical camps and loan facilities. SRF strongly believe in Corporate Social Responsibility (CSR). I never thought a profit-making enterprise would provide water pump to villages, conduct eye camps, diabetic camps, blood donation camps and even create HIV awareness among surrounding villages.

Finally, I got to see the factory. The whole process is automatic and the raw material is nylon. It is woven just in the way a fabric is. Then it is passed through ammonia to give it more strength. The smell of ammonia was nauseating and gave me a headache. The final product is then given a colour, as desired by the customer and the fabric is then tested for tear and hardness.

The factory resembled a park. There were more than 50 peacocks over there. I took many pictures with the peacocks.

Amman Steel

When I studied linear expansion in Physics, where bars could be made into wires, it sounded more fiction than fact. Amman Steel proved me wrong. The raw material (billets) come all the way from Andhra Pradesh and are heated in a coal fired furnace at 1600 C.

The heat was unbearable and I wondered how the workers worked all day long. The steel rods were then extruded in stages through an automatic process. The whole operation looked scary and I felt I was witnessing the last scene of 'Terminator' in which Arnold Schwarzenegger and the villain fight beside the furnace. The sounds in the shop floor would have made a very good background score for the movie 'The Matrix'. The Manager warned me not to go anywhere near the steel. He mentioned cases where the arms and legs of the workers had to be amputated, merely because they came in contact with the molten steel.

The steel is cooled, cut and packed. Nearly one lakh litres of Cauvery water is used to cool the steel. A startling piece of information was that none of the 500 workers are from Tamil Nadu. They were either from Bihar or Odisha and were contract labourers. I was shocked. Tamilians, possibly with the largesse and freebies from the Tamil Nadu State Government are not willing to endure hardships any longer.

SOLAR Farm

Melting polar ice caps, rising sea levels, floods in Dubai, Srinagar, and Chennai are happening during our times. The planet has to be saved. A couple of TEDTalks impressed me. One of them was by the Prime Minister of Bhutan. I learned that Bhutan is the only 'Carbon Negative' country in the world. The other project was about soft drink bottles filled with water, being inserted in roof tops, thus saving precious energy during the day. I saw a similar design in Trichy. An apartment was completely lit by solar power during the day time. The man behind this is Mr. Arun Rebero. A man on a mission, he showed me how he installed solar heaters in hospitals. He took me to a village, Puthanampatti, which is around 40 kilometres from Trichy, where an entire college (Nehru Memorial College) was being powered with solar energy. Arun uncle explained about Azimuth angle, how solar panels are designed and how they function in the control room.

It was a beautiful business model, where the business man would invest in solar and save on taxes and also get a huge depreciation. Arun uncle explained that one solar powered house could save 20,000 trees. Unfortunately, many small players provide shoddy equipment to reduce initial cost and people are losing their trust in solar power.

One point about uncle impressed me very much. His passion for solar power has made him travel across the world, study various systems and get all the international certifications possible. In fact, uncle was designing a solar powered car for Dr. A. P. J. Abdul Kalam. But sadly before he could complete the project, Dr. Kalam passed away.

BPO at Nehru Memorial college, Puthanampatti

I also got an opportunity to observe the functioning of a BPO (medical transcription), which was the captive unit of Nehru Memorial College, Puthanampatti. The employees here are mostly students from the college and a few educated people from the neighbouring villages. Brilliant! The students are able to earn some income which can finance their education and the villagers do not have to run to the neighbouring towns in search of jobs.

LivPET

Which is the first large scale PET bottle manufacturer in India? Who supplies bottles to J&J and Bovonto Kalimark? It is a company called LivPET.

Before going to the factory I went on Wikipedia to memorise the formula, density, melting point, boiling point, and thermal conductivity of polyethylene tetrachloride. I was even updated about Young's Modulus, tensile strength, elastic limit and notch test. I thought I could exhibit my knowledge and show off. But the humility of Ms. Sanjana who is the daughter of Mr. Ramanan (CMD LivPET) and the magnificence of LivPET humbled me. She took me around the shop floor and patiently explained the entire process.

Fifty machines of different shapes and sizes, a couple of dedicated workers for each machine and perfect management was a spectacle to be observed. There was not a speck of dust in the factory and the whole place looked like a work of art. Everyone was focused on their job. The workers are handpicked from the villages nearby and groomed to become skilled artisans.

LivPET is an example of how a small town entrepreneur with a big vision can set up a world class industry.

Xtra Reinforced Plastic Private Limited

Have you seen the movie 'Zoo Keeper' starring Kevin James? There are four golf carts used in the movie. These were supplied by this company. This company is located in one of the suburbs of Bengaluru, Kacharakanahalli. It is celebrating its 50th year of commencement. So, what's the big deal? Our Prime Minister Modiji would be impressed with what is happening there. Arnold Schwarzenegger happens to be one of their customers. This company supplies golf carts to a dozen countries.

Bosch wanted to prove that their power drill could propel a car. The company took up the challenge and created a prototype. In this unit, they make 65 different models of golf carts.

In the factory, I saw different moulds, the assembling of the unit and the final testing. The raw material used is fibre reinforced plastics. When TATA Motors and Titan (Tanishq) wanted to celebrate, they approached Mr. Zarryl Lobo, who with his ingenuity, made a gold gilded Nano car. India must be having a lot of talent. If only they could be recognised and marketed, could we be on our way to beat China? I thank my uncle Mr. Shane Lobo, who took me around the factory and showed me their working.

Ashtanga Ayurvedics Pvt. Ltd.

With greenery all around, this place looked like a mini forest. No, I'm not describing my visit to the Sunderbans forest. The place is Ashtanga Ayurvedics factory. Here more than 100 products, right from shampoo to cosmetics to health drinks and chyawanprash are made. One of the partners, Sasi uncle took me around. Though he is 52, he doesn't not look a day older than 30. He kept smiling all the time and was bursting with energy. Ayurveda must be doing the trick!

He showed me the inventories, the process and testing system. The employees have been working here for years. Who could leave such a loving person? Uncle said that one of his biggest challenges was product costing. Thanks to the plethora of raw materials and products, the amount of money which went into the making of a product had to be minutely calculated.

Sashi uncle took one product and showed the calculations. Costing includes raw material cost, labour, taxes, transportation charges, electricity bill and land bill. These costs get apportioned into that one product which is manufactured in bulk. The cost varies from product to product. I learnt about ABC (Activity Based Costing) which is very important for the pricing of a product.

This unit was started in 1936 by Shri K. S. Varrier, an ayurvedic doctor, with his wife. The couple would prepare about 50 drugs at home. Shri K. S. Varrier had a shop on NSB Road, the lifeline of Trichy. Initially, no customer came to his shop. Those days when marketing was unheard of, he hit upon a novel idea. He kept betel leaves outside his shop and the day's newspaper on the table. On seeing them, customers would be lured into his shop. Shri K. S. Varrier would start a conversation with them on health and ayurveda and gradually, make them his customers. Thus was born Ashtanga.

BABY Industries

Thuvakudi lies in the suburbs of Trichy, close to BHEL factory. This place is populated with ancillary industries to which BHEL outsources its jobs. The times ahead are tough for many of them as BHEL has been bearing the onslaught of competition from China. One such company is Baby Industries.

It's a 40 year old company. In spite of challenging times, the owner of Baby Industries is smart. Rajesh uncle, a chirpy man with a sweet smile, has razor sharp eyes. His success mantra; look out for new customers. Fertilizer plants, sugar units, you name them, his marketing team is there. The feather in his cap is the order from Hyderabad Metro to make the fabrications for the railway platforms.

I observed 50 ton cranes in the manufacturing bay. There are two such bays which were 100 metres long each. The processes depend on the carbon content in the steel. The drilling machines are computerised. The machine which impressed me the most was the one that could bend the entire beam to the desired angle. I understood fabrication well. Use the right grade of steel, deploy cranes to lift them, drill and weld them at the right locations, bend them at the appropriate angles and test them for strength. Rajesh uncle mentioned that they use Rockwell Hardness Testing. Hold it! It's not over! The biggest challenge lies in shipping them back to the customer's destination. It's an extremely arduous task.

Interestingly, Rajesh uncle has also diversified into the cake business and runs a chain of cake shops called 'Cake Bee'. Uncle also shared one of his keys to success. He holds memberships in Indo German Chamber of Commerce, Indo European Chamber of Commerce, Indo American Chamber of Commerce and even Indo Gulf Chamber of Commerce. This enables him to visit different countries, attend conferences and update himself on latest technologies. He is also an active member of CII (Confederation of Indian Industries).

Visiting many industries has given me a broader perspective. I can now comprehend how Maths, Physics and Chemistry can be transformed into technology. I can also perceive how people come together and convert technology into a profitable enterprise.

Notes from the parents:

Every year, we come across unnerving incidences of students committing suicide. We treat each incident separately. But isn't there a common thread connecting them all?

We perceive that these students felt helpless, hopeless and were in total despair. They thought that suicide was the only option. They were like race horses with their blinkers on. They could only see in one direction and did not have a broader vision.

They could not see possibilities. The book 'Possibility Thinking' by Robert Schuller was invigorating.

Nick Vujicic is a great example of possibility. He was born without hands and legs, but that did not deter him. Today, he is a motivational speaker, author, swimmer and a family man.

One of our former students, attempted to commit suicide because she got one percent less than the cut off medical marks. We made her *see other possibilities* and today she works for Rolls Royce. Her family is proud of her.

This was one of the prime reasons why we supported Sagarikka's USY project. Whenever she faces tough situations in future, she would *see other possibilities.*

THE KALEIDOSCOPIC EXPERIENCES

This chapter is about the different experiences which I have not been able to fit into any category

It is show time folks!

On 22nd July, 2015 Mr. Yoagandran, a friend of ours and former student of TRICHY PLUS, arranged for me to observe a day's film shooting. He discontinued his Engineering to pursue a Film and Media course from Whistling Woods, Mumbai. He is a graduate in Visual communication from SRM University, Chennai. He has worked for many reputed Media firms like UTV and SUN TV. Currently he runs his own production studio in Chennai.

The location for the shooting was Rakshith Hospital, Chennai. Just as I was about to reach the spot, I received a call. It was from Rakshitha, a girl who lives down our street. What was interesting was that we had never spoken to her before and she just happened to call. I don't know what this phenomenon is called. Dad says, it is synchronicity.

At the shooting spot, I was introduced to Director Sasi who has directed Tamil movies like Sollamale, Roja Kootam, Dyshum and Poo. The movie, which was being shot, was 'Pichaikkaran' (The Beggar). The scene was about a police inspector beating up the hero, in front of the hospital. 'Take 1'. Sasi uncle was not satisfied. He and the hero (Mr. Vijay Antony) would check the shot in the monitor. And then there was 'Take 2'. They were still not satisfied, and then 'Take 3', then 4, then 5 and on it went. The heat was scorching and the crew stood under the hot sun. It took more than three hours to shoot just a minute's sequence. I was dehydrated and wanted to throw up. Sasi uncle would come to me after every shot and show me the monitor and describe each shot. He introduced me to the members of the crew. In between the takes, we would sit down under a tree and talk.

Sasi uncle said that his biggest strength was that he could visualise every scene, how the words had to flow out from the actor, their body language and how the set should be. He would keep taking the shot till he got what he had visualised. He would keep watching the monitor till the picture he saw on the screen matched his visualisation. He said anyone with this kind of a memory could become a successful director. This was great advice!

There were 200 people on the set. About 120 of them were supporting artistes getting Rs.600 a day, hardly doing anything. That makes it a total of Rs.72,000. The senior supporting artistes would make Rs.2000 a day. Their work… nothing. They would sit under the shade of the tree, drinking tea, eating and chatting. Every time the shot was ready, they would come and stand in various positions. I made a quick mental calculation that it would cost up to two lakhs rupees for a day of shooting. Sasi uncle said that a low budget movie would take three months to complete. That would be a whopping two crores. And then you would have to pay the stars, the Director and the Music Director. Add to that the cost of editing and screenplay. I guess, a low budget movie would cost at least ten crores.

Sasi uncle asked me to join him for lunch. The lunch consisted of two non- vegetarian dishes and was delicious. I wondered at so much expenditure, just to take a single shot of a policeman beating up the hero.

Sasi uncle took me inside a caravan to meet actor-music director Mr. Vijay Antony. He was very cordial. He said that he got the last rank till class 12 and had 22 arrears in college. He started comprehending the meaning of life only after college. Vijay uncle said that getting educated is a waste of time and believed that students would amount to nothing, if they had no passion. He figures that we need four things to succeed in life. Learn music, know an additional language, learn finance and be health conscious. He was then attending finance classes to upgrade his knowledge. His daughter was studying in class 2 and he wanted to stop her studies after class 5 as he believes that home schooling is the key to success.

There are a few take aways from this experience. A Director should have the power to visualise every shot even before the first scene is shot. Watching on the big screen is cool, but making of the movie is a painful and difficult task. Successful people are very kind, loving and humble.

As I am writing this book now, on 3rd May, 2016, Pichaikkaran is running to full houses. The movie has already crossed its 50th day and is a box office hit. I wish I had requested Sasi uncle to allow me to play a small part in the movie. That could have made me quite popular.

Isha talks

Isha foundation is a non-profit organization founded by Sadhguru. It is spread world wide and as I mentioned earlier we had visited Mount Kailash with the Isha group.

During our trip to Kailash, we used to have satsangs every evening. The guruji would play a video of Sadhguru every day. I took an instant liking for Swami ji and wished to meet him in person in the future.

Before leaving for Lake Manasarovar, we stopped at Taklakot. Our rooms at Taklakot, Tibet were bad. There was just one caretaker for the entire hotel. There was no room service, no waiters, no receptionist... nobody. It was freezing but the faucets were leaking and hot water would be supplied only for one hour in the morning and for one hour in the evening. at freezing temperatures. Our attitude began to dip, but Sadhguru's video that very evening made us see the lighter side.

He recounted the tale of an American lady who went to one of these Chinese hotels and asked for a room. They asked her whether she wanted a yellow room, white room or red room. She asked what the yellow room meant. The reply was there would be a leakage in the bathroom. The lady then asked what the white room meant. The reply was, the bulbs would not work. When she finally asked what the red room meant. They mentioned that the commodes could not be flushed. After listening to this story, we were grateful that our rooms were much better.

Sadhguru's talks on Lord Shiva were captivating. Do you know what happens to your body when you are near Kailash? Sadhguru said, your Swathistana chakra (Seat of will power and digestion) and your Ajna chakra (intellect or third eye) will get activated.

He said that Manasarovar is a lab to create life. Beneath the lake are the blue coloured rocks. From these rocks, comes blue light. Higher minds can see forms. They resembled a man below the navel and woman above the navel. Guruji trapped a genie in himself to gather the experience, but ended up burning his intestines.

I never knew that Lord Shiva had no parentage. There are no records of his birth or death. It is believed that Shiva is an alien from outer space. Parvathi took a fascination for him and wanted to marry him. Shiva and his retinue of ganas (demented people) came for the marriage. Shiva was smeared with ash. The hideous sight of him made Parvathi's mother faint. Parvathi pleaded that he change his form. She could accept him in any form, but her parents couldn't. Shiva then transformed himself into the virile and handsome Soma, whom Parvathi's mother accepted.

Sadhguru asked us to give a thought about why Shiva and Parvathi could not bear children. Lord Ganesh was a manifestation of Parvathi and Karthikeya sprung out of six children who were put together by the apsaras. These apsaras had been impregnated because of the virile sperms of Lord Shiva which floated down the river which no earthly mother could bear. Sadhguru said that the pebbles in Kailash could not be explained by volcanic or tectonic theories. It could have been formed only by meteorites. A meteorite of that size would have destroyed the earth. It is said that Shiva used to take 12 year breaks. Could he have gone during one of these periods to outer space with his ganas, regulated the speed of the meteorite and made it safely land on Earth, thereby saving the world? Was this the beginning of Mount Kailash?

On the southern phase of Mount Kailash you would see steps right from the top to the bottom. Sadhguru said that Ravana once came to meet Lord Shiva and pay his respects. Ravana was a doyen in music. He started singing and had Lord Shiva in raptures. Meanwhile, Ravana started climbing up the peak to meet the Lord. Parvathi was disturbed to see this man enter her abode without their permission. She kicked him down the hill. As Ravana fell, his drum rubbed against the mountain, thus creating the steps from the top to the bottom.

Could there be more to this story then what meets the eye? Lord Shiva does not seem to be a mythological character. He seems to be a mystical character!

IIT coaching institutes

I have always noticed that the customer is treated as a king in my Dad's office. He always tells his staff to smile, greet the customer and find out their needs.

In this regard, I want to share some interesting experiences which occurred when I went for the NASSCOM conference in Chennai on the 23rd and 24th of July, 2015. The conference got over by 4 pm and we booked an OLA cab. We were in search of a few IIT Coaching Institutes in Anna Nagar. On our way my dad contacted one Aakash Institute. He spoke to an official and asked for a few details about IIT coaching. The phone got disconnected and within a couple of minutes, it rang again. A gentleman from Aakash, Delhi office called and spoke to my dad about the coaching details. My dad wanted a demonstration video and the gentleman said that he would send the link to dad's email immediately, which he did in the next two minutes. I now understand why Aakash is one of the premier coaching centres in the country. Their response was prompt.

After half an hour, we reached another IIT coaching institute. The entrance of the building was fancy. The interiors were lavish with rich, ornate and showy furniture. There were impressive posters everywhere. The entire ambience was proof that the fees would be very high. At the entrance there were two sturdy bodyguards. I wondered, what could people steal from an institute? We were instructed to write our name, phone number and address in the log book.

There was a classy and stylish receptionist inside. She looked at us as though, she was looking at a wall. We gave her an apologetic glance as we tiptoed into the counselling room. It was a room on the first floor. There was a stern looking lady inside. We perceived that she was highly disturbed that we came at such an unearthly hour (5pm).She barked at us to wait outside. With feelings of guilt, we sat on the edge of a sofa. How could I make it to IIT without her support? My very life depended on her. We were scared to even inhale deeply, lest the high priestess got upset with us and the dream of my IIT got squashed. We waited for 20 minutes with bated breath as Her Highness continued with her office work. We felt like poor miserable souls. It was like waiting for Lord Yama to give us permission to enter the gates of heaven. Madam continued with her office work, oblivious to our presence.

After completing her work, Her Highness looked at me and beckoned me inside with her index finger. The moment had arrived. In the counselling room, there were only two chairs for the three of us. Being the little one in the room, the onus was on me to bring a chair from outside. It was not customer service. It was the customer, servicing.

Her Highness (the counsellor) asked me for my mark sheet. I said that I hadn't brought it. She sternly asked me why not and I apologised for the grave error. Then my dad told her about my one year break. She interrupted dad and said a student of my calibre would not be permitted inside the portals of such a great institution. My dreams of IIT vaporised instantly. Should I fall at Her Highness's feet and plead with her? Her Highness was kind enough to suggest that we could go and meet the Director in the next room and grovel. Through the glass pane, I could see the Director looking seriously at the ceiling fan; possibly he was doing some angular momentum calculations!

Then it was dad's turn; he was all fire and brimstone at the behaviour. He gave that lady a piece of his mind. I wish I had recorded the talk. It would have been a wonderful script for the movies.

This institute has missed a great student.

A customer may be a king, but when it comes to IIT coaching, the institute is the king.

Choice of schools: International vs. Open school

We went on a trip to Bengaluru and Hosur. Our objective was to survey schools which could satisfy my appetite. We examined three schools in Bengaluru, Mallya Aditi International School, Canadian International School and Stonehill International School. Unlike schools in my town, where the Principals' shout at you and staff look at you with contempt, the International schools have a touch of professionalism. They welcomed me with open arms. I was given a presentation on the school which was full of video testimonials on how the school could transform my life. We were then taken on a trip around the school in a golf cart. The playgrounds were 10 times the size of the playgrounds you would find in the schools of Trichy. The schools had swimming pools, basketball courts and gymnasium unlike many of the schools I have seen. The dining halls were a class by themselves. The rooms were spotless and exquisite. The classrooms were spacious. Each student had a desk to himself and the students were mostly expatriates and from well to do families. I made up my mind. If I had to study, then this would be the place. But my parents wanted me to explore more before I could make up my mind.

We then drove to Hosur. Our destination; Arohi Open School. We went into the deep interiors of Hosur. We passed TVS Suzuki Factory and many other industrial units. We crossed the school twice without noticing its existence. Finally, we landed up at its gate. Many stray dogs gathered around us and started barking ferociously. We thought of turning back, when a handsome man approached us with a bright smile on his face. He welcomed us and took us in. I was expecting to see a school. But there was none. There was a two storeyed house and a hut nearby. The building was in the middle of nowhere, with acres of space all around. It was surrounded by trees. The air was fresh and the atmosphere pleasant. The gentleman introduced himself as Mr. Ratnesh. He's an IIM Lucknow graduate. His passion: to make children explore the world on their own terms. He was all alone in the building as the kids had left on a field trip.

I asked uncle, what was the age limit for joining this school, how many classes were there, section, and all the stupid questions I could ask. Ratnesh uncle said that any one from the age of 5 to 99 can study in that school. There are no classes, sections or syllabus. He said "The world, he said is the syllabus."

I couldn't believe that such a school existed on this planet. If a child wanted to learn music, he was free to do it. If the child then wanted to shift to painting or carpentry, he was welcomed. Every week, they would have jaunts to the villages where they would study the history of that place. Uncle shared that most of the villagers were millet cultivators because of water scarcity, but later shifted over to rice cultivation because of the policy of the Government. The excursions also included rock climbing and studying the mud, at the bottom of the lakes. Climbing trees was part of their curriculum. Resource persons included watchmakers and architects. I saw a hut built with clay and leaves. The entire construction and design was done by the children. They had to fill water from a hand pump. Every bucket and mug had a label indicating its capacity. The idea was to instil the thought of water conservation among these youngsters.

Uncle said that the children discovered Archimedes Principle through experimentation. They had built rafts and tied petrol cans beneath them. Each can could displace 20 kilograms of water. If a man who weighs 80 kilos were to stand on the raft, four petrol cans would be required to prevent him from sinking.

It was a WOW and AHA experience. I wish to spend more time in this school. I dream of establishing a school like this in my town, where children would need no formal education and no thought control.

A great day at the Visvesvaraya Museum but for...

The Visvesvaraya Industrial and Technological Museum is located near Cubbon Park, Bengaluru. I reached the museum with Dad and Mom at 9 am in the morning. I thought that we would be among the first to reach the museum, but there were hordes of people waiting outside.

We went to the Chemistry section first. We saw an exhibit of zinc and copper plates, which were dipped in acid and transmitted current. I got an idea about the principles of Electrochemistry.

The Physics section had the exhibits of the diodes and triodes. Models of coal plant and nuclear power plants helped me to figure out how electricity is generated. A display of Fleming's Left Hand Rule gave me a hang of how two vectors, current and magnetic field produced a third vector force perpendicular to them. I was able to make sense of how motors work.

The most absorbing demonstration was how a parabola functions. A room had two parabolic devices at either ends. They were each one metre above the ground. I stood at the focus of one mirror and whispered "Life is beautiful". Dad who was at the other end could hear me say that. I was bewildered. The sound waves from the parabola were not disturbed by the hundreds of people in the room. The demonstration of a Whimhurst's Machine collecting charges like a dipole till it ended up in an electric discharge was fascinating. Shows of the lighter and the darker shadow, how conductors, semi-conductors and insulators work, Lissajou's Figures, persistence of vision, laminar and turbulent flow were captivating.

I was able to get a grasp of how Doppler Effect predicts weather. The frequency is high when clouds approach and higher when clouds move away from us. The exhibit on AND, OR, NOR and NAND gate had a wow effect on me. I was able to assimilate the fact that the internet works on fibre optics. Messages get conveyed over thousands of miles purely by internal reflection of laser light. The analogue signal gets converted into a binary code and transmitted. The ground floor at the cross sections of the diesel engine, internal mechanism of clock, pelton turbine and the rotary engine. There were prototypes of different levers.

This museum is a paradise for Math buffs. I came out with a clear understanding of normal distribution curve and Reynold's Number. Even Bernoulli's Principle and what makes a plane take off were clearly explained over here.

This museum is a great place to be in. It was an incredible and stupendous experience. The work done is mind blowing and formidable. When so much of energy and effort has gone into making this masterpiece, couldn't the authorities keep the toilets clean?

THE TOILETS IN THE VISVESVARAYA INDUSTRIAL AND TECHNOLOGICAL MUSEUM WERE REEKING.

The stench was terrible. The stink, miasma and effluvium were so strong that I had to hold my nostrils every time. The malodour made me want to puke. It is a shame and a disgrace that these authorities who are paid with the tax payers' money don't even bother to keep the toilets clean. If this is the state of affairs in a National Monument which has thousands of visitors even on a working day, how will our dream of Swachh Bharath get fulfilled? I want the authorities to apologize and devote the rest of the lives to at least keeping the toilets clean. This will help more children come here to develop their minds without having to bother about the bad smell.

Notes from the parents:

Jim Dornan – the founder of Network 21 and one of our role models, once shared a story from stage. This is about how the *Chinese bamboo* is cultivated. The farmer plants the sapling, waters and nurtures it. One year of diligent effort and the sapling doesn't grow an inch. The farmer doesn't lose his patience and keeps nurturing it till the fifth year.

The indolent bamboo tree wakes up from its slumber after five years. It grows at an alarming rate and reaches a height of 80 feet in just three months. Jim told us that, the tree was not dormant for five years. It was actually building a strong foundation, which would support the tree, once it grew to a height of 80 feet.

Aren't children like the *Chinese bamboo*? We have personally come across numerous examples from our town Trichy. Dhaarini Srinivasan had to surmount all odds but she persevered and later on, went to the extent of working at the United Nations in Geneva. Dhildar Niyaz had barely cleared his 12th standard Maths paper, but dreamt of cracking the CAT exam. This young man persisted and cleared his CAT exam in his fourth attempt and went on to study in IIM Kolkatta. Maheswari is the daughter of a bus driver. She had a dream of doing her Masters in the USA. Her visa was rejected four times. Today she is the best outgoing student from her University in Connecticut, USA.

Pappu is also like the *Chinese bamboo,* she will grow at her own pace. We are aware that we are like the Chinese farmer whose only job is to water, nurture and allow it to grow.

MEETING PEOPLE

- PEOPLE WITH DIFFERENCE
- POWER OF ASSOCIATION - MEETING PEOPLE
- THE THIRD PILLAR OF DEMOCRACY
- ATTENDING CONFERENCES

PEOPLE WITH DIFFERENCE

My parents have been conducting a programme called VERBO-CITY LIFE for many years. My first project in USY was to attend this workshop. During this course, I went on many field trips.

Once a man asked God, "Why did you create so much of pain and misery in this world? How are we going to eradicate this pain?"

God said, "That's why I created you"

What could be more true? I saw many people doing their best for the society. Here are the true accounts of four such people who have made a difference to Trichy through their institutions.

Pravaag (A school for the Autistic and the Dyslexic children)

When I hear the word "Autism", I recall the movie 'Rainman'. Here, Dustin Hoffman, who plays the brother of Tom Cruise, is autistic. He cannot reciprocate love, but he has an uncanny ability to crunch numbers. He can memorise the entire telephone directory overnight.

I saw a girl in Pravaag with the same ability. She was detached, but could paint a picture in two minutes. There was a kid screaming all the time. Even our presence was highly disturbing. I am told that even Sachin Tendulkar and A. R. Rahman had traits of autism.

Dyslexia is a well known word. Remember the movie 'Taare Zameen Par', where Ishaan Awasthi sees images that are laterally inverted. His teacher, Ram Shankar Nikumb explains his inability with an apple. He says, when you hear the word apple, you associate it with a picture, sensation, smell, taste and sound. Dyslexics don't have this ability. Pravaag has well equipped labs to integrate the senses. They also have a lab to improve the motor skills of children. There is an activity filled park attached to the school. We had a great time with these kids over there. One kid in particular took a liking for me and would not let me go.

Unlike normal schools where teachers specialise in putting the children down, the teachers here keep appreciating them. They were a paragon of patience and the children would repeat the activity over and over and the teachers would keep rectifying their mistakes. All this is happening because of the vision of the Ramanujam family. Mr. Ramanujam, has made it the mission of his life, to plant trees and stop global warming. Mrs. Geetha Ramanujam has made it her mission to look after these children. I always used to think that profit should be the motive behind any business. But the Ramanujams taught me, that service to the world could be the biggest motive anyone could have.

A special mention about the parents. The parents bring the children to the school in the morning and are ready to take them back in the evening. I met a mother whose two children are Mentally challenged and studying in the same school. Her husband works in Dubai. She is an embodiment of love and sacrifice. These parents never go out on holidays. They don't even go for movies as these children would not be able to sit through them. Geetha aunty had once organised a fashion show for the mothers. Many mothers cried because that was the first time they had applied make-up in many years.

One day a mother asked God, "There are so many beautiful, intelligent, smart and competitive children in this world. Then, why did you send this child to me?"

God replied, "This is my special child. It is the one closest to me. I was looking for the mother who would look after it the best; that is why I chose you."

Shanthivanam (Home for the Psychologically challenged destitutes)

Remember the movie "Deewangee", in which Ajay Devgan has a split personality? He is not aware of committing a crime when he is in the other state. There is also the Tamil movie "Anniyan", in which actor Vikram plays the role of an avenger, a Romeo and a tax paying citizen, all in one. This symptom is called 'Schizophrenia'.

Think of being with dozens of such people. This is what we experienced at Shanthivanam. There was an MBBS student, who had a split personality. Another individual was extremely pious, but could become volatile with shift in personality. Radha had been physically abused and was a victim of flesh trade. Unable to bear the stress, Radha became a schizophrenic. She would talk about being in the USA and then talk about life in Mumbai, possibly places she had never visited but wanted to fantasize about. There was yet another lady, who could end up convincing me that she was in touch with ghosts and evil spirits.

You must have also heard about the Tamil movie 'Moonu' with Dhanush in the lead. Let me give you a cue. The song 'Why this Kolavari' was in this movie. Dhanush is a patient with bipolar disorder which would cause mood swings. Sometimes the patient could become extremely violent or even have suicidal tendencies. Shanthivanam is a place filled with such people. There is a huge fencing around this building to prevent the inmates from escaping.

Jothi was deserted by her family. She was found lying on a railway platform with no place to go. Shanthivanam took her in and rehabilitated her. Many of the occupants have been abandoned by their families. The kindness of Dr. Ramakrishnan, a leading psychiatrist was instrumental in building this home. Shanthivanam trains its inmates on making paper plates, cups, pillow covers, bed sheets and vermicompost. They also generate their own milk. The dung of the cows is used for producing biogas, which powers the kitchen. Can you believe it is a self sustaining model with Psychologically challenged destitutes?

LEED (Home for the transgender and sexually deviant)

These people frequent the traffic signals and moving trains. The very sight of them used to irk me. Now I had the unique opportunity of interacting with a dozen of them within closed doors. Our team comprised 15 students.

Their team comprised five transgenders, three bisexuals, a couple of gays and lesbians. Initially I felt very uncomfortable and I wanted to run away from that place.

The LEED team spoke to us and gave us numerous examples from Hindu mythology of Lord Vishnu being a transgender and the importance of Thirunangai (transgender) in our culture. Some of them explained that they were exploited as young boys which made them different. I became aware that sexual orientation in these cases is by choice.

Many of them were extremely talented. They could sing very well. Some of them were adept dancers and one person was a mimicry expert. One of them had even participated in the popular TV program Airtel Super Singer contest. They were highly proficient and made excellent rangoli. They explained about section 377 and asked us to fight for their rights.

Hats off to Radha aunty, the founder of LEED. She is a courageous and outspoken women and from a well to do family. In spite of facing numerous obstacles Radha aunty decided to fight for the rights of the third gender. I admire her zeal and determination.

ORBIT - Organisation for Rehabilitation of the Blind (A factory for the differently abled)

What I witnessed here seemed to be right out of Ripley's Believe It Or Not. It's a factory where all the workers are either visually impaired or physically challenged. ORBIT is an ancillary unit of BHEL. It is run by a trust that had the vision to rebuild the lives of the physically challenged. ORBIT is the brainchild of Dr. Joseph

Gnanadickam an opthalmologist who dedicated his life for the rehabilitation of the visually challenged persons.

These people primarily do the pressing and punching of components. Two people work per machine. The physically challenged person sets up the component and gives a signal. The visually challenged person operates the machine.

The coordination between them is excellent. There are nearly a hundred people working in this unit. They have been getting orders from other industries as well. Their quarters are attached to the unit and in spite of all the challenges they face; they have been able to support their families.

I once read a story about a tourist who visited hell and heaven. In hell, he found that all amenities were provided. There were hotels, parks, theatres and shopping malls. But these people looked sad and frail. On enquiring further, he found out that they could not bend the elbows of their hand. Though food was kept on their plate, this deformity kept them from eating. The tourist then went to heaven. He found the same facilities there also. He noticed that these inhabitants also could not bend their elbows but they looked happy and healthy. He witnessed that they made a circular formation at the dinner table. The first one would feed the next, the next would feed the very next and so on and all of them ate their fill. ORBIT is the very same heaven on earth.

These four experiences have instilled a belief in me that the purpose of life is to serve. We, as a team pledged that we would commit ourselves to the service of mankind.

Notes from the parents:

It was our fault entirely.

I was consumed with my business. Transforming the minds of the youth and generating money in the process was my priority. The evenings that I was free, I would devote it to Rotary, Toastmasters, book club and other social events. Savitri, an avid Rotarian, had dedicated herself to the cause of Rotary. We used to get back home by 9 pm, and then we would eat and go to sleep. The one who was left in the lurch was Pappu. No wonder that reflected in her tenth standard marks. We made a firm decision after Pappu's tenth to follow the *Principle of Exclusion*.

The principle states – '*Get rid of what you don't want to make room for what you want*'. We got this idea from Skip Ross, the author of 'Say Yes to your Potential'.

It was a firm 'NO' to our business and taking classes in the evening. We were back home by 6 pm. During Pappu's USY, all our social activities took a backseat. We had to even avoid important marriages, family functions and get-togethers.

From 6 to 11 in the night, it was Pappu all the way. The evenings consisted of teaching her Math, Science, Current Affairs, Reading Newspapers, watching and listening to Motivational Talks and assisting her with her Vocabulary. We would then plan for the next day and check out whether our activities matched our goals.

We had to get rid of many things to make the most important part in our life work - 'Pappu'.

POWER OF ASSOCIATION - MEETING PEOPLE

"Hang out with people who are smarter than you, you'll see the difference." During my USY, I inculcated a habit of meeting successful people. Initially, I was very shy. I thought that these people are so great that they would not be interested in talking to a small girl like me, but I was totally wrong. These winners were very open. They shared ideas, gave me tips and each experience was invigorating. When you surround yourself with great people, they will lift you higher. They were professionals, businessmen and students.

Meeting Professionals

Major General Ian Cardozo – 'I cut off my own leg'

I met the Major General at a hotel in Bengaluru. He had a strong and determined look about him. I smiled at him and he smiled back. That is how our conversation started. What he shared, shocked me out of my wits.

Major General Ian Cardozo was a young major in the 5 Gorkha Rifles. He had fought in 3 wars, Indo-China War (1962), Indo-Pak War (1965) and Indo-Pak War (1971).

In the 1971 War, the fourth battalion of the Gorkha Rifles did a heliborn operation. They went in by helicopter behind the enemy in an air field called Selat. There were only 484 people and were told that there were only 200 irregular enemy soldiers in Selat. The battalion was also informed that they would get support within eight hours and therefore, didn't take much food. The food supplies did not reach them for the next 48 hours. The fight ensued for 10 days and finally, the Pakistanis surrendered.

By this time, the battalion's number was reduced to 452 people. To their amusement, the soldiers later found out that the Pakistanis were 10,000 in number. The then Defence Minister of India, Babu Jagjivan Ram had made an unintentional error. He announced that a brigade had reached Selat. A brigade consists of many battalions. The Pakistanis, who had eavesdropped on the conversation, thought that they were outnumbered. They surrendered and then realised, to their bewilderment, that they had been fighting only 450 soldiers.

And then, a drama in real life took place. Major General Cardozo stepped onto a mine which shattered his leg. He asked the doctor for morphine but it was out of stock. He asked whether they had any pethidine. He then requested the doctor to cut off the shattered leg. The doctor said that he didn't have any instrument. He asked his batman for his khukri and instructed him to cut off his leg, but the batman refused.

That was when Major General said "Give the khukri to me." He cut his own leg off and ordered "Now go and bury it."

Major General was taken to a hospital in Pakistan and had to be operated on by a Pakistani doctor. He told his commanding officer that he did not want a Pakistani to operate on him as he did not want Pakistani blood on him. His commanding officer told him that he was a fool. Major General said, "I am prepared to die a fool than have Pakistani blood on me." Finally, he was operated on by a Pakistani surgeon Major Mohamed Basheer, to whom he is grateful to this day.

Today, Major General Cardozo runs, walks and swims. On the January 17, 2016, he participated in a 11 kilometre marathon in Mumbai with his artificial limbs.

I wondered, where this man got so much courage? What kept him going at this age when others would have prefered to relax and play with their grandkids?

Major General Cardozo read my mind. He looked at me with his piercing eyes, smiled and said "Battles are won or lost in the mind, before they are won or lost on the ground."

Ms. Lisette Geers – Heal the World, Make it a Better Place

Lisette Geers is from The Netherlands. She is six feet tall and was working as a Business Development Consultant for a college, in her country, when she discovered her true calling - 'yoga'. She had come to India to learn about Ayurveda. She spoke about food ranging from chocolate to Hagelslag. Interestingly, potato is the staple food of her country. Just as we mix vegetables with rice in our country, in Holland they mix vegetables with potato. She spoke about the windmills of her country and quipped that there was no one there to operate them. Temperatures here drop to -10 degrees in winter and eight degrees is considered as lovely weather. People cycle all over the country (no wonder they are healthy) and sometimes enter Belgium, France or Germany which are the neighbouring countries. Lisette spoke about drugs and prostitutes for which Netherlands is infamous. She correlated that drugs and prostitution could be the reason for the high crime rate in her country. When I asked her what she felt about the refugee crisis in Europe, she said that people should be more sensitive to the needs of the world and embrace the Syrian refugees who are pouring into Europe.

When I shared about my sabbatical with Lisette, she was very appreciative. She said that the broader our spectrum, the more energy we can find within ourselves. Thus, I could discover my true purpose and give energy to the world.

Mr. Veera Sekar – Upanishads and Rock Art

Mr. Veera Sekar worked for BHEL and is the author of the book "Rock Art in Kizhvali". He cited numerous examples and illustrated the connection between rock art and Upanishads. It was an eye opener and a completely new subject for me.

Veera uncle also mentioned about the value system during the days of the Chola kings. When the government allocated shops, for every six shops given to the Hindu community, four were given to the Muslims. He also spoke about The Jewellers' Oath. They had to take an oath every three days to avoid unscrupulous practice. The oath was taken every three days, so that the thought was firmly imprinted in the minds of the goldsmiths.

Meeting Businessmen

Mr. Ramanan (CMD, LivPET)

On 6th September, I went to Mr. Ramanan's house. It is a mansion with several rooms, that I almost got lost in it. It is very convenient to play hide and seek there! Their kitchen is probably as big as our house.

Mr. Ramanan is a leading entrepreneur in Trichy. He is the pioneer of the PET bottle revolution in India and started his factory way back in the 1980s.

Ramanan uncle had worked under Dr. Abdul Kalam. They were working on a project to make pure hydrogen. He remarked that Dr. Kalam was a great leader and knew how to manage men and resources. He firmly stated that every citizen should pay his or her tax. Many people complain that the Government does not provide us with benefits and hence, we need not pay our taxes. But, Ramanan uncle insisted that it is our duty to pay our taxes. What impressed me the most was that, to date uncle has never offered any bribe.

Uncle gets up at 4.30 in the morning and reads seven newspapers everyday to keep himself up to date with the current affairs. He has no lateral entry in his company. He grooms his team right from the beginning and does not allow the culture of his company to be adulterated by outside elements. He is not only interested in their work from 9 to 5 but also in their family from 5 to 9. He believes in work life balance. He talks to the families of the employees because he believes that his employees should be human beings first then productive workers. No wonder, many of his employees have been with him for over 20 years.

Uncle stated that the integrity in family life is of utmost importance. He also said that the strength of our culture lies in respecting our parents. At every opportunity, he spoke with high regards for his father, who was instrumental in introducing the concept of outsourcing in BHEL. When his mother was not well, he was always by her side in the hospital for two whole months.

Uncle said that vision is a moving target. The world will be different next week from what it is this week. So we need to keep on updating, fine tuning or even changing our vision if necessary. Uncle said that youngsters should shift from IT to core sector to propel 'Make in India' towards success. He said that many Indian companies should enter the defence sector to save precious foreign exchange.

Mr. Ravi Murrugaiah (Promoter, Vasan Real Estates)

Ravi uncle is a leading businessman and owns a real estate business. Ravi uncle's house is like a palace with a cricket ground in it. There were a row of cars in the garage. I sat in the plush drawing room and interviewed Ravi uncle. He was very warm and gave no indication of being one of the most successful businessmen in Trichy. He made me feel at home.

Uncle said that before promoting a plot, they had to take account of the roads that would cut across the plot. He had to apportion 33 percent of the space for roads. Another 15 percent to 20 percent of the land had to be allocated for other purposes. This left him with only 50 percent of the land on which he had to work out his projects. His strategy is to choose land just outside Corporation limit and inside Panchayath limits. This made the land affordable for middle class and upper middle class buyers. If the real estate is close to the Corporation, people have easy access to schools, hospitals, restaurants, bus terminals and railway station. In fact, two of his prime projects are at a distance of 5 to 10 kilometres from the heart of the town.

Ravi uncle's vision is to make Trichy the second most important city after Coimbatore, leave alone Chennai. He is on a mission to create satellite towns around Trichy. He was of the firm conviction that people need individual houses and not concrete jungles to live in. He affirmed that this would save the environment and make the city a better place to live in.

Mr. Leo Ananth (Chairman, eQuadriga Software)

Mr. Leo worked in Germany where he met his partner, who gave him the idea of starting a business in India. His portfolio includes HR, Billing, ERP products and website development. He mainly recruits people through employee reference and trains his team through mentoring concept, where a senior employee mentors a fresh employee. Performance appraisal is done on a yearly basis. The performance of the company, team and individual are given a weightage of 40:30:30. He explained about employment time tracking, payroll management, leave management and attendance management. Uncle explained the difference between the German market and Indian market. Germans give importance to quality and are professional. Indians give importance to price and nothing else. Leo uncle mentioned that when he was young, he had no family commitments and could dare to fail. Now, the commitments were much more and he was scared. I was reminded of Jack Ma's statement, "From 20 to 30, you make mistakes. From 30 to 40, you work for yourself. From 40 to 50, work on your strengths only. From 50 to 60, work for the young and after 60 you relax."

I spoke to many more entrepreneurs like Mr. Clements, a dealer in Bosch power tools. He gave me an insight into the power tools industries.

Ms. Anuradha Sivakumar, the proprietrix of Sai School,Lalgudi. She explained in detail about school management.

Mr. Kanagasabapathy, Chairman of TIIC (Tamil Nadu Industries Investment Corporation) who explained how they help start-up industrialists.

Meeting Students

Ms. Padmasini Veerabadran (Architect, Germany) – "Children should have a say in their life"

I always wondered why Germans are so intelligent and well-known. Albert Einstein, Beethoven, Bach, Adolf Hitler, Werner Heisenberg, JohannesGutenberg, Anne Frank and Ferdinand Porsche were all Germans. I think I have the answer.

I interviewed Ms. Padma. She had studied at SASTRA and did her post graduation in Germany. She did her MS on Natural Hazards and Risks in Structural Engineering. At present, she is working and doing projects on seismic waves and their effects.

Excerpts from what she spoke about Germany:

Education - Germans are very strong in their basics and concepts. Indian students have great difficulty in coping up with studies here. This is because we are spoon-fed and have no understanding of concepts.

Festivals - The 'Oktober BeerFest' is the main attraction. People buy a litre of beer for eight Euros. This festival generates huge revenues for the country.

Freedom- Parents don't interfere with the career choice of their children. Children are free to choose their careers.

Travel - Padma shared a wonderful experience of travelling to Lapland in the North Pole. Lapland is famous for Santa Claus, reindeer and sleigh dogs. She also watched the dazzling of the skies due to the intense magnetic field at the poles. This phenomenon is known as Aurora Borealis.

Industry - Germans are the best engineers in the world. It is astounding to know that this small country has some of the most powerful manufacturing companies in the world. Adidas is world number one in apparel and accessories. BASF, the chemical giant, Bayer, the household name in pharmaceuticals , Carlz Zeiss, the dream of any photographer, Mercedez, Grundig, Henkel, Knorr, Lufthansa Airlines, Puma, Bosch, Siemens, Volkswagen, Porsche and BMW are all German companies.

Food - People are extremely health conscious and avoid fried and junk food. They have salads, toast, rolls and diet on a regular basis.

Corruption - Corruption is absent in Germany. If citizens want a document, they have to get the appointment through internet and present themselves to the authorities at the stipulated time. The paper would be passed as per the rules of law. The word bribe is unheard of... but Padma has heard rumours of corruption at high levels.

Disadvantages of being in Germany-a medical prescription is mandatory to buy any medicine for which a doctor has to be consulted. For this consultation, the patient has to obtain an appointment a week in advance.

People are very sensitive here. Lawn moving, switching on grinders and all forms of 'Noise making' should be done only between 9 and 11 am. How boring... Imagine what fun we have in India - blaring speakers in the middle of the night, running drilling machines in the early hours of the morning, honking our automobiles and scaring old people and school kids! When will the Germans understand these pleasures of life?

Padma mentioned an Indian family who had lived in Germany for 18 years. Their toilet was partitioned from their neighbour's bedroom by a wall. At midnight, when this family had to answer the call of nature, they had to inevitably flush the toilet. This 'extra-terrestrial' sound highly disturbed the neighbour forcing them to complain to the authorities. The family had to take remedial measures.

I met a girl who wants to become an author and study Genetic engineering, but her parents want her to choose a career of their choice.

MY QUESTION: What makes the parents expert in every field? I went to the Hindu Lit Fest where I saw hundreds of budding authors. I have also come across students who have great interest about gene banking and stem cell research.

But here are some parents interfering with the thoughts, dreams and passions of the child. If India wants to be a great country, it needs people who can think on their own.

Germany with a population of 82 million is one of the most powerful countries in the world. It is a member of G8. Tamil Nadu has got a population of 72 million and we can't even handle a flood. The reason is we don't have independent thinkers. Tamil Nadu and India will succeed the day, 'Parents stop interfering with the decisions and choices their children make.'

"If 82 million can do it, then why can't 1252 million do it?"

Ms. B. Dharrini (IIT AIR 26) – A girl with a dream cannot be denied

I met Dharrini's parents in Chennai. Her father Mr. Bala happened to invite us to their house on our return from Mount. Kailash. Her proud mother is a Bank Manager. She said that Dharrini did not prepare for her IIT exams from any acclaimed coaching institute but when Dharrini got the all India rank, one well known institute utilised her name for roping in fresh students. Dharrini would cycle to one Professor's house to learn Maths, to another Professor's house to learn physics and to yet another Professor's residence to learn chemistry. She made it very clear to her parents that she would focus only on IIT entrance and not her CBSE exams. Even the day before the exam, Dharrini was reading Tamil cine magazines. Such was her confidence, as she was very strong in her concepts. She was an ace quizzer, writer, painter and traveller in school. Her role models are Indra Nooyi and Steve Jobs. She is now happily settled in USA.

Ms. Vigneshwari Subramanian (PHD – Bio computation, Helsinki, Finland) – I spent a week with 30 Noble Prize winners

Vigneshwari did not get into MBBS because she missed the cut off mark by 1 percent. She took a year break for writing medical entrance tests, when she found her true calling; Bioinformatics. She did her Masters in Finland because education is good and free there. She did her PhD in bio computational methods.

She currently works for a pharmaceutical company. The company gets orders to design selective drugs for protein targets, which are usually cancer molecules, diseases or diabetes. From a million molecules, Vigneshwari has to choose 100 molecules, which will be the most effective, using computational methods. For this, she needs the knowledge of Molecular Biology, Chemistry, Computers and Statistics. The molecule is then given to the chemists who would then test it on guinea pigs.

Vigneshwari is currently working on stem cell research. Stem cell can be regenerated into any organ, heart, lungs, liver, etc. This regeneration is done in a petri dish. In my innocence, I asked her how they form a heart or liver in the petri dish. Do they shout heart... and it becomes a heart? She burst into peels of laughter. It was possibly the funniest thing she had ever heard in her life. She then explained that organ regeneration is done through a process.

She said that the quality of Indian medicines is not upto the mark. The paracetamol from Finland has more efficacy than that of India. She said that many Indian products are getting banned in Europe because of poor quality. Even our Alphonso mangoes are not accepted there.

Every year, 30 Noble Laureates meet at Lindau. These Noble Laureates spend the whole week with the best students from Europe discussing medicine and physiology. Vigneshwari was selected from Finland and had a mind boggling week with the greatest of the great.

I met many such students. Prominent among them are:

Mr. Giridhar Raghunathan, a Tissue Engineer from Canada, who is into Nanotechnology and Nanofabrication. He is currently working on replacing skin tissues with polystyrene. He is also working on replacing damaged blood vessels. Currently he lives in Quebec and is a student at University of Laval, Canada.

Mr. Aswin Varrier studied theatre arts in Christ College, Bengaluru and is involved in scripting, production, direction and acting. He is on a mission to promote theater art throughout India.

Ms. Sona Kumaresan from IIM – Ahmedabad, shared her insights on life there. The students here hardly sleep for two to three hours per day. The institute has a Marketing Fair called 'Insights'. Towards the end of the course the students can choose from three companies during their placement season. Sona is currently with Samsung Electronics.

Mr. Koushik Raju of Bishop Heber College, Trichy, is the Youth Ambassador from India at the United Nations. He has started a NGO in Trichy to rehabilitate prostitutes. For this, he was given an award by Prime Minister Sri Narendra Modi. Though he is a young college student, he also runs a consultancy through which he guides and supports small businessmen in Trichy.

Mr. Narendra Babu works on logistics in Singapore. He is also a marathon runner and a regular at the Singapore marathon. Naren has completed Logistics & Supply Chain Management Programme from Curtin University, Singapore.

Mr. Karthik Semban is a nanotechnologist in the USA. He has completed his M.S. from University of New Haven, Connecticut.

Mr. Prabhakar has completed his MBA from the USA. He has specialized in the field of Finance. All of them shared their views and perspectives with me. I am grateful to them for broadening my vision.

Notes from the parents:

An experiment was once conducted. Two groups of children were asked to solve the same jigsaw puzzle. The only difference was, one group was shown the final picture and the other group was not. The group which was shown the end picture was able to solve the puzzle much faster.

Adi Godrej once said, the secret of success was not to put the present forward...but to put the future backward...*Begin with an end in mind.*

We implanted this idea in the mind of one of our students, Vinoth. He wanted to pursue his mechanical engineering from NIT. We asked him to go through the entire syllabus and find out how each subject would be applicable in real life. How each subject could be converted to cash? Our objective was to make him *begin with the end in mind.* Vinoth earnestly followed our suggestion and went on to become a topper in his group. Today, he works for Volkswagen in Germany.

If Pappu wanted to become an IAS officer, we wanted her to see the end picture in the Collector's office. If she wanted to be a hotelier, we wanted her to see the end picture of how a hotel worked. If she wanted to see a BPO, we wanted her to see the end picture of a BPO. If she wanted to become a Doctor, we wanted her to see how a hospital functions. If she wanted to become a movie maker, we wished for her to see how the movie industry works. If she wanted to be a stock broker, we wanted her to experience the same.

THE THIRD PILLAR OF DEMOCRACY

Mr. John Benedict (a former student of my dad) works as an IT consultant for the Karnataka High Court. Mr. John a broad-shouldered, serious looking man, is constantly focused and has passion written all over him.

Mr. John was a student of St. Joseph's College, Trichy. He worked in CTS and then started an NGO in Palakkad, Kerala which today supports 300+ children in their education. After a stint with Tripura police, where he enabled their connectivity, he moved over to Bengaluru to cleanse the legal system.

One particular incident moved him – an elderly lady in her 70s had been visiting her advocate continuously for two years over land litigation. She had paid her advocate two lakhs from her paltry savings. Much to her dismay, the advocate had already made a deal with the defendent and the case had been closed more than two years ago. The lady was unaware of the happenings. Mr. John has taken up this case to bring justice to the old lady.

A similar story was recounted by Mr. John, where an elderly man had been dealt with similarly by his lawyer. It took this man 20 years to realise that his lawyer had conned him.

John anna noticed that the legal system was in deep malaise and needed help. There are 18,000 cases pending in Karnataka

Appellate Tribunal. Corporates don't pay taxes and when slapped a fine, get away with a stay order. More than Rs 1,39,000 crores (two years Karnataka budget) is under litigation. If this money is paid to the government, wouldn't this largely benefit the citizens of Karnataka?

Filing a case and getting receipt is a manual and time consuming process.

All files have a physical copy stored in rooms (I witnessed the storage). It is appalling that there is no inventory system or storage management. It takes weeks to retrieve a document (God save India!).

There is no system of sequencing or scheduling and cases are handled ad hoc.

When the judges need additional information, the whole system is so decrepit; it takes a huge amount of time to retrieve the necessary files.

No wonder with such a legal system, India is chugging at snail's pace.

The solution is 'Digitisation and IT'. John anna and his team are working at a frenetic pace at digitizing all the records. John anna is also working on a multitude of other projects. One of them is video conferencing between the jail and court. I was rattled on discovering that many jail inhabitants continue being in jail even after serving their sentence.

India needs many more John Benedicts to save this country. I wish all of us have the same passion to bring in 'Acche Din'. John F Kennedy said, "Ask not what the country can do for you, ask what you can do for the country". Kudos John anna for the service you have rendered to India!

John anna took us inside the High Court in Bengaluru where the public are not allowed. Thanks to John anna, I got the opportunity to enter the courtroom and watch the proceedings. I was surprised to find the courtroom very different from what I see in the movies. It was all high tech and the room was air conditioned. There were several rooms in the premises and many proceedings were happening simultaneously.

From here, I was taken to another chamber where I was introduced to a High Court judge. I was inspired by this towering personality. I had to pinch myself that I was face to face with a High Court judge. He shared his experiences with me for the next 20 minutes. It was amazing.

The Judge narrated that, till his eighth grade, he had to sit on the ground in his school. He studied in a Kannada medium till his tenth standard. In his first job, he got an allowance of Rs 5 per day. Within 2 years his salary increased to Rs 5000 per month.

He had the dream of becoming a judge. To become a judge, command over English was mandatory, but he knew only Kannada. He resolved not to speak in Kannada and decided to speak only in English. Even after becoming a judge, he maintains his resolve. He spoke to me in flawless English.

He shared his experience on how he passed a "death sentence". The accused worked in a government job and had killed his entire family, including his two daughters. It was a premeditated murder. After much deliberation and contemplation, the judge decided to pass the death sentence. He stated that a mother gives life and only God has the right to take one's life. He said that he had to invoke God's blessings to enact this sentence.

He also explained to me the meaning of corruption. He said, "If your dad gives you Rs.100 to buy a notebook and instead you buy an ice cream, that is corruption." That was when I realised the exact meaning of corruption. The misuse of anything is corruption.

I also met the famous Judge John De Cunha and got the opportunity to listen to him for a few minutes. I asked him what gave him the courage to make tough decisions. The judge stated that he gets courage during tough times because of the black robe he wears. The black robe gives him the strength to differentiate the right from the wrong. This robe makes it an obligation for him to protect the Constitution. When I asked him for advice, he asked me to be passionate about whatever I do.

I have a great regards for the judges. They uphold the Indian Constitution; but one thing disturbs me. Every judge has an escort who walks in front of him on the corridors of the High Court. They shoo people away and insist the people should stand up and move aside when the judge walks by. Why should the world's greatest democracy have a feudalistic mindset?

Notes from the parents:

Selling Amway products was perhaps one of the best experiences that Pappu had. She faced rejection after rejection. But somewhere deep inside she learnt that rejections are a pathway to an order. Pappu learnt *delayed gratification*. Earlier, she would want instant gratification. If she wanted an ice cream, it was 'NOW".

This was the greatest transformation that we saw in Pappu. We are reminded of the famous marshmallow test.

A group of junior school kids in Singapore were offered marshmallows. They had a choice of grabbing marshmallows then and there or wait for an hour to get two marshmallows. Most of the children grabbed one and ran away. Very few waited patiently for an hour. These children were tracked after 20 years. The first group were leading ordinary lives. The second group, the kids who were ready to wait for one hour, were leading lives of significance.

The other learning that Pappu derived from her AMWAY experience was to be "*thick skinned and to be independent of the opinion of others.*"

Once our neighbour came to our office during Pappu's USY. She was in a state of discomfort as she had found Pappu talking to her teenage son. We knew that our daughter is equally comfortable talking to both boys and girls, but we did not want to argue with our neighbour. We shared with Pappu what had transpired. To our surprise, she did not react to the situation and took it in a positive sense. She just stopped talking to the boy as his mother did not appreciate it.

We now realize that our daughter had became *thick skinned and independent of the opinion of others.*

ATTENDING CONFERENCES

NASSCOM

The National Association of Software and Services companies is a non-profit organisation. It was established in 1988 in India and is a trade association of BPO and IT industries.

On 23rd July, 2015, I attended a NASSCOM conference. It was conducted in ITC - Grand Chola, Chennai. The hotel was luxurious and splendid. I saw a lot of prominent people over there. I started taking photos all around. At the reception of the summit, I was surprised to see dozens of counters. The conference hall was posh and could seat 700 people. The stage was grand and well-lit. There were a couple of giant screens on either side of the stage. Each participant was impeccably dressed. The men wore suits, well polished shoes and carried leather bags. The women were classy and spoke with an accent.

The morning session was gibberish to me. I heard words like assignable projects, contingent work, performance review process, team-based activities and aligning with milestones. An international speaker spoke about, how the world was changing. All the time, I kept hearing words like scale, form, leverage, processes and practices. The main theme of the summit was The Digital Highway: HR's Journey into the Future. I badly needed a break. In the break, I went and started taking pictures. There was a model of a bus, beautiful paintings, a replica of the petrol gas station and a cut out of a truck. My best hideout was Chotu Chaiwala, where attractive cups and kettles were displayed.

Again another session started. This was about digital conservatives vs. digital cowboys, digital Darwinism, rivers meandering, digital natives, HR disruption blah blah blah… I got a severe headache. Why did mom and dad have to bring me to this place? I badly wanted to go back to school. I thought my teachers were more interesting.

The lunch was the most exciting part of the conference. Throughout the morning session, more than half the audience was outside the auditorium. But during lunch time, the attendance was 100 percent. I had soup, pulav, pastas, salads, a variety of chicken dishes and finally, hot gulab jamuns, jalebis, pudding and ice cream.

Finally, the conference started making some sense. Mr. Ajay Kaul, the CEO of Jubilant Foodworks spoke. I understood what he said because I'm a regular at Dominos Pizza. Mr. Ajay said their mantra is Make it… Bake it… Take it… Even the top brass at Dominos had to work at a store. He spoke about how college students, who work on a part-time basis, get trained. He also talked about the happiness score and satisfaction index of the customer. He added that Dominos could deliver Pizzas anywhere in India within half an hour of a call. I badly wanted to ask him a question and stood up. All the 700 people looked at me. They wondered how this kid was allowed to enter the conference room. My hands started shaking and I could hear my heartbeat. I said, "Uncle, it's raining, the roads are blocked and there is a traffic jam. How do you ensure that the pizza is delivered in 30 minutes?" Uncle said "If I answer this question, you could easily come and sit in my place. It's not a coke and churan formula that I can explain. It involves a lot of six sigma processes that is difficult to explain." I came to the conclusion that eating pizza was easier than making or selling it.

Perhaps, the best speaker was David Sturt, the author of Great Work. He shared a beautiful quote of Albert Einstein, "If I had an hour to solve a problem and my life depended on it, I would use the first 55 minutes determining the proper question to ask, for once I know the proper question, I could solve the problem in less than five minutes." I wish my teachers would see this quote. They never gave me time to even think while solving a problem.

Mr. David shared many examples. He spoke about Mr. Marty Cooper who worked at Motorola. Mr. Marty asked himself a question, "Why is it that when I want to call a person, I have to call a place?" This led to the invention of the cell phone. He shared another illustration. A team at IDEO Company wanted to design a better stroller to carry children. Instead of sitting in the board room and having a discussion, the team was asked to go out into the field and take pictures. The team came back with the pictures of how strollers got caught in cracks, how the mothers had to hold the baby on their hips to unfold the stroller and how bags and purses had to be put on top of the baby for want of storage space. They came up with a new design and solved all these problems in one shot.

Mr. David shared another superb example. There was a hospital for children, where seven children had died during operations in one year. The hospital authorities knew that they needed better coordination during the operation, but did not know how to do it. They asked for help from a Formula 1 race maintenance team. This team had the calibre of changing the tyres and rectifying the racing car in seven seconds. The racing team made alterations to the process at the hospital operation theatre. No child died in the operation theatre after that. I understood that change lies in talking to the outer circle. The hospital authorities did not consult other hospitals. The problem to their solution was given by a Formula 1 team.

The highlight of the conference was the talk given by chess supremo Viswanathan Anand.

Chess, according to Viswanathan, was the Science of understanding patterns. When he was asked what motivated him, he said that he first mastered the opening and end games. The minute differences that he learnt later motivated him and drove him to perfection.

Mr. Anand said that after playing professional chess for four decades, he still had a lot of unlearning to do as the game was getting transformed. He sighted an example of 'Sicilian Defence' and how it kept getting modified. He compared it to getting fluent in a language where one had to keep practising and see how others use it.

Mr. Anand spoke about mental barriers. He said that Russia had produced hundreds of grandmasters, but India had to wait till 1987 to get its first one. Once he became the grandmaster, the barrier was broken. Today, India has 39 grandmasters.

Once he became a grandmaster, he could not win for the next six months. This was because he did not know what to do next after reaching his target. The same complacency set in him after his world championship titles in 2007 and 2012 His spirit was willing but his flesh was weak and the desire was burning out. He advised that, once a goal is reached, we should look out for the next goal. Viswanathan said that he learnt much more from failure than from success. He said that failure forced him to learn.

When asked on whether he was disappointed on losing to Magnus Carlsen, the champ retorted that it was a great learning opportunity and he understood how the young minds in the game operate. He said that young minds were more flexible, knew how to bluff in the game and didn't carry any baggage. He said that he accepted his failure. He jocularly remarked that the only disappointing aspect was that, it had happened in Chennai.

Viswanathan said that in chess you have to keep yourself updated. The game is not the same as it was 30 years ago and that's because of computers. Understanding new stuff was a bit uncomfortable for him.

Finally, the audience asked him a lot of questions. One person asked him how he prepared himself after a defeat. Viswanathan replied that when he lost a game, the most important thing for him was to sleep well. He would go to the gym, run for an hour, shower, have dinner and sleep. This made him mentally ready for the next game. He also stated that success lay in team work. His team would double check his opponent's weakness, do detective work and then plan on what surprises to come up with.

When another member asked him the purpose of his life, Viswanathan said that he never gave a thought to such heavy questions. Viswanathan said "I don't play chess because I want to win the world title, I want to win the world title because I want to play chess"

I was the last person to ask him a question. I was feeling exalted, face to face with the World Champion and asking him a question. My question was, "The other two C's in India, cricket and cinema, give the players an iconic status. But chess players are not treated as celebrities. So do you have any regrets?" He said "No, not at all. I enjoy playing chess and frankly I feel that I have been rewarded enough for that." He then shared an incident. He was once at the Chennai airport getting his baggage cleared. One of the travellers kept looking at him repeatedly. He could kind of figure out who Viswanathan was but could not place him properly. Viswanathan felt pleased at being sort of recognised. Then the man went up to him and told him in Tamil "Sir, you acted very well in your last movie" Viswanathan then went and related this incident to his wife who said "You should have asked the person which movie was it, and whether he recognised you as the hero or the villain."

I had recorded his talk and listened to it a dozen times. It gave me a great opportunity to understand how a champion thinks.

The Hindu Lit For Life

It started in Nov. 2010. The idea was to celebrate the 20th anniversary of *literary review* a supplement of The Hindu, which is devoted to books and literature. This is an annual event held in Chennai for three days.

My calendar was booked on January 16th and 17th. I attended The Hindu Lit For Life at Sir Mutha Venkatasubba, Rao Concert Hall, Harrington Road, Chennai. I missed the day one of the festival and felt very bad about the same. The theme of the festival was 'Get Inkspired'. There was a huge board where people could write the name of the best book they have read and liked. I saw a seven-year-old kid write 'Harry Potter'. I was embarrassed as I have not read the entire series of Harry Potter. I wanted to show off and wrote Jonathan Livingstone by Richard Bach on the board. I had only seen the cover of this book. I saw a desk with some very old books. The person at the desk told me that he was on a mission to save these books and asked me whether I was willing to adopt one of them. I wanted to contribute to this cause, but in future with my own money.

The first speaker I witnessed was Mr. Alexander McCall Smith. He has authored more than thirty books. I was hearing about him for the first time. His stories were about a fictitious character Madame Precious Ramotswe, who runs a detective agency in Botswana. Mr. Alexander mentioned that he wrote an average of 3000 words a day. It was at this point that I decided that one day I would write a book. After his talk, I rushed outside to take a picture with him.

I then listened to an inspiring talk by Lionel Shriver. She is the author of "We need to talk about *Kevin*" which is now a movie. There was a lot of psycho stuff which I could not comprehend. She spoke about the difficulty she had in bonding with her son and how her son grew up to be a sociopath. I found it all mumbo jumbo, but kept taking notes. One thing I liked about what she said was, "Happiness is getting up in the morning knowing what to do"

Then it was time to listen to Mr. Shashi Tharoor. He talked about India and the networked world. He explained globalisation with a simple analogy. "An English princess with a Welsh title leaves a French hotel with her Egyptian companion, who has supplanted a Pakistani; she is driven in a German car with a Dutch engine, by a Belgian chauffeur full of Scottish whisky; they are chased by Italian paparazzi, on Japanese motorcycles into a Swiss built tunnel and crashed. A rescue is attempted by an American doctor, using Brazilian medicines and the story is being told to you by an

Indian from Thiruvananthapuram". He was referring to the death of Princess Diana. He spoke about Jihad vs. McDonalds and how India is a multi aligned country. Mr. Shashi Tharoor impressed me a lot with his command over the language and his knowledge on diverse topics. After his talk, I rushed out to take a photo with him. I also met his son Kanishk Tharoor, who was so handsome and cute that I had no other choice but to rush to the book stall and buy his book. I have his book in my house but have still not opened it!

In the evening, I listened to Chinmayi, who is a popular playback singer. She spoke about the Chennai floods and what action should be taken if they recur in future. I took a picture with her. She was gorgeous and very attractive.

Next morning, I observed a panel discussion. The panellists were Mr. Ninan (Former Editor of The Economic Times), Mr. Dulat (Former RAW Chief), Ms. Jayanthi Natarajan (Former Environment Minister), Mr. Shashi Tharoor and Mr. N. Ram (Editor – The Hindu). The topic was *Making India Work.*

Mr. N. Ram quoted R. K. Narayanan and said 'India will move on'. Mr. Shashi Tharoor said "Our government is like a doctor who can diagnose the disease but can't cure the patient." He also said that our bureaucrats work very hard but the PMO (Prime Minister's Office) is like the Bermuda Triangle, where files vanish and no action takes place. He joked that our economy grows at night when the government sleeps.

Mr. Tharoor explained the difference between China and India. In China, if they wanted to make a six lane highway, they would draw a line on the map and bulldoze their way through. In India, if they wanted to make a two lane road, somebody would get a stay order from the court, some union activist would protest and sit in the middle of the road and some actor would fast to gain publicity. He was also positive and said that 17 percent of the people in India were literate at the time of Independence, today it is 65 percent.

Then, Mr. Dulat spoke about the Kejriwal factor and said that India was working. Mr. Ninan said that India was a big thunder with a few rain drops. He said that 20,000 crores have been wasted on Air India in a country which has scarce resources.

A major learning for me from Mr. Ninan was: China, Japan and Korea focussed for 20 years on education. Today, these countries are fully literate and India is 30 years behind them.

Ms. Jayanthi Natarajan was very passionate in her views. She revealed a very important piece of information that NABARD found that bread making is the largest job providing industry in India but we focused on producing more engineers. She said government hospitals have 9000 procedures for billing, but not one procedure of taking care of patients after they are discharged from the hospital. She was outraged that nobody in the Parliament cared about the Chennai floods. The Parliamentarians were discussing nonsensical issues when people in Chennai were dying. Now I became a fan of Ms. Jayanthi Natarajan and rushed to take a photo with her.

In the afternoon, the discussion was about a book written by Ms. Barkha Dutt called *Unquiet Land.* The panellist who interviewed her was Ms. Anitha Ratnam, who was very charming and charismatic. I had seen her in the movie 'Boys' and 'Kandukonden Kandukonden'. She looked even more beautiful in person. Ms. Barkha Dutt is the most powerful and energetic woman I had ever seen. She had once gone from Egypt to Libya without papers and ducked bullets to cover a piece of news. Once she sat on top of a car and forced the person sitting inside to come out and give an interview. She forced her way into Kargil to cover the news about the Indo- Pak war. This was later made into a Bollywood movie called 'Lakshya' with Preity Zinta in the lead role. Barkha Dutt shared a funny anecdote. Preity asked Barkha, "What clothes did she wear during her 15-day-stay in Kargil." Barkha mentioned that she wore the same shirt, pants and underwear on all the days. Then Preity asked her about the makeup she wore.

Barkha said that this is a man's world. Whenever men use bad language with her, she takes it as a compliment. She must be a very thick-skinned woman and I want to be like that. A young boy asked her a question, "What would happen if Modi, Rahul and Kejriwal joined hands and got together?" Ms. Barkha paused, smiled and replied "Have you heard of John Lennon's song, Imagine?"

Another gentleman quipped, "Do you want to be like Arnab Goswami, who is at one end of the spectrum or Karan Thapar, who is at the other end of the spectrum in news reporting?" Barkha replied, "I wish to be myself."

Another lady said that in those days there used to be 1.30 news and 9 o'clock news. Is it necessary to have 24×7 news channels? Barkha said that today news is available instantly on Facebook and Twitter. She asked the lady, "Do you think people watch the 9 o' clock news for information? NO! They watch it for entertainment." I realised that this woman is unlike normal human beings who lead predictable lives. She is relentless, obsessed and consumed in the pursuit of news. She has many haters. There was misinformation of her being married to a Kashmiri Muslim. There were also rumours spread that she used an iridium phone which led to the death of three Army jawans in Kargil. There is also a Facebook page which spreads negative information about her and even asked people to give her book a one star rating. This is a woman of steel, she just moves on.

I was so captivated by her that I wanted a picture with her very badly. I rushed behind her till the very exit but she was constantly surrounded by people. I could not meet her that day and was depressed. She is my hero.

The final session was with Amish Tripathi. He had come to promote his book 'Scion of Ikshvaku.' I had never shown any interest in mythology earlier. I had only sketchy information about 'The Ramayana' and 'The Mahabharata.'

Mr. Amish mentioned that, as soon as he opens the laptop to write a book, he feels that he is not a writer, but an instrument through which the book is being written. He said Brahman is the source of everything. Infinite wisdom flows from the universe, through his pen into the book. His job is only to let it flow.

He explained the difference between masculine and feminine with a brilliant analogy. In China, before the Beijing Olympics, the Chinese were trained on what clothing to wear and also given instructions on how to shake hands with foreigners. The hand shake had to be for exactly three seconds: no more, no less. Less duration would communicate lack of bonding and excess duration would be offensive. They were also given strict guidelines about the colour of the shoes and socks. It had to be strictly black shoes and white socks. What did the Chinese do? They complied with the instruction. China is a masculine society. Amish asked, "What would have happened if the similar guidelines have been given in India?" We would have done the opposite. Indians would have worn black socks and white shoes for the next one year. India is a feminine society!

He was then asked why his stories did not have a happy ending. Mr. Amish said that happy ending is a western concept. In 'The Ramayana', the story did not end with Ram and Sita coming from the forest. Sita was sent away by Ram, and finally consumed by Mother Earth. Lord Ram, full of remorse committed Jal Samadhi in the River Sarayu while chanting… Sita, Sita, Sita. Even in 'The Mahabharata', The Pandavas went to heaven and found The Kauravas were already there. Mr. Amish said that in Indian mythology, there is no good or evil. Our stories are not meant to give us a good time; our stories are there for questions to be asked. Question comes from the word quest. Our stories are a quest to quench our thirst.

We went to meet Mr. Amish backstage after the talk. My mom wanted him to autograph the copy of her book 'Scion of Ikshvaku'. He took one look at the book and said that it was pirated. My mother showed the bill which was in her cell phone. She had purchased the book from one of the most famous online retailers in India. A pirated version of the book had been sold by them. It was a very embarrassing moment both for Mr. Amish and my mother.

CII (Confederation of Indian Industries) Seminar

I attended a one day CII seminar at Hotel Sangam, Trichy. The topic of this seminar was 'Skilling India.'

A consultant spoke about Saint Gobain, the leading glass manufacturer. It runs a glass academy. I absorbed that this company trains unemployed youth, rural youth and college graduates about the glass industry. They are later absorbed into facade making and manufacturing varieties of glasses.

The Head of Welding Research Institute, BHEL, broached on the topic how youth are trained and inducted into various welding jobs. I was moved by one story. A welder had lost his hand in an accident. This accident did not deter him from doing his job. He found an innovative method by which he could weld with only one hand. From this example, I learnt that anything is possible if one has the desire to do it.

One thought kept troubling me throughout the seminar. I had read an article in The Hindu that the future belongs to automation and robots. The article stated that skilled workers would be unnecessary in the future. I asked the experts on stage to comment on this article. They replied that they did not see it occurring in India for the next 20 years.

At lunch time, I approached and spoke to the Director of NIT, Trichy. I shared with him about my USY project and my one year break from school. He did not appreciate the idea. He is entitled to his opinion.

MMA (Madras Management Association) Seminar

Formerly known as the Madras Institute of Management, MMA was founded in August 1956. In 1957 the name was changed from MIM to MMA. MMA has a Trichy chapter. My parents are members of this Association. On August 25th, 2015, I got an opportunity to attend one of their seminars.

As I was going to the seminar on the evening, a sombre incident took place. Our driver met with a minor accident just outside the venue. A young man cut across the road on his bike without giving the slightest of indication. This person did not have even a single scratch on his body, but a huge crowd gathered. The crowd started attacking and abusing my driver. The person involved in the accident wanted to apologise and leave the spot because he knew it was his fault. This boy was not even wearing a helmet and had crossed from the wrong side of the road. What irritated me was that the crowd seemed interested in looting us. I was surprised that there were so many people standing there with nothing else to do. They asked a traffic policeman standing over there to ask us for a bribe. Never in my wildest of dreams would I have thought that the public would encourage the police to take a bribe. Surprisingly, the policeman said, "I am a government servant. They give me salary. Why should I take a bribe?" This policeman is my hero.

The speaker at MMA was Professor R. Sridharan Ph.D., Independent Educator and Consultant from Melbourne University, Australia. The talk was on the four mantras of business. The mantras were Effectiveness, Efficiency, Handling Uncertainty and Variability.

There was a Q & A session. There were nearly 40 students from IIM- Trichy, 40 college heads and a few businessmen in the hall. I mustered all my courage and asked why students abroad were encouraged to work while studying, but students in India keep studying without any work experience. The Professor appreciated me for having the guts to ask this question. After the meeting he came and personally met me and gave me a lot of ideas. I felt elated that he preferred to talk to me, rather than the businessmen and the students of IIM. I was too excited that evening.

IIM (Indian Institute of Management)

I was a visitor at ARCTURUS event at IIM-Trichy (A premier Management Institute of India)

The first event I attended was a presentation by students on buying stocks. One team made financial projections about Infosys. They said that the share price of Infosys would increase from Rs.1,400 to Rs.2,100 in the next five years. Another team said that the share price of Tata Motors would increase from Rs.360 to Rs.420 in one year. I heard new terms like CAPEX, discounted cash flow, billing rates, rate of salary increase, potential in different markets, growth in the IT industry, historical evaluation and SAAS. I realised that I understood very little about stocks. I then walked into the conference hall. Somebody was giving a talk on Teach India. I wanted to interact with the students but everyone seemed busy, so I went back home.

The Trichy Book Club

The club was formed more than 30 years ago for book lovers to meet up and review books. The only rule is that the review should be in English. Ms. Prema Nandakumar (a literary critic), Mr. Diljit Shah (Gopaldas Jewellers) and Brig. Narayana Swamy are the important members of this reading group.

We are fortunate to have a club like this in our town. Every month a book is reviewed. The speakers are of the highest class and one can meet many literary aficionados here.

The Gochala Trail

The first review I attended was a travelogue.

The Ramanans shared about their travels on the Gochala trail. I was transported to another world through their communication, photographs and videos. There were three speakers. Ms. Vrinda Ramanan, who was very bubbly and friendly, Mr. Ramanan, a very serious and a soft spoken man and Mr. Mahesh Khanna who was very energetic.

They spoke about Sikkim. I have been to Sikkim but when they spoke about it, it sounded different. They described colourful rhododendrons, oak trees, flowers and the path to heaven. The photographs shown by Ramanan uncle of Kangchenjunga were breathtaking.

That was the time when the earthquake occurred in Nepal in 2015. The trekking team felt the tremors halfway through the journey. The porters demanded more money and refused to go ahead if not paid more. But Ramanan uncle was firm. He told the porters, that he would not pay a single paisa if they did not complete the journey. The porters had to yield. I then realised the power of decision-making.

Vrinda aunty mentioned that they could not perceive the intensity of the earthquake in the mountains. It was only in the plains of Kathmandu that the severity was felt. She showed a scary photograph. They had to cross a small bridge, three feet wide. This bridge was made of logs. While going up the mountain there was no water beneath the bridge. While returning, the river was running rapidly underneath. The water was very close to them and one slip into the waters would have meant instant death.

Fortunately, all the trekkers returned safely.

Vrinda aunty shared Joyce Kilmer's famous lines, "*Poems are made by me, only God can make a tree.*"

Review of '*The Silent House*' by Orhan Pamuk:

The review was done by Dr. Bennett, who is a Professor of English in National College, Trichy. He is a very warm and well-read human being. He has read 64 Noble Prize winning books and dreams of reading them all.

Before reviewing the book, Dr. Bennett gave us an understanding of Turkey's history. Till the 3rd century AD, Turkey was known as the Byzantine Empire. It was later called Constantinople and was the heart of Christianity. In 1400 AD, Turkey was captured by the Seljuk Turks and called the Ottoman Empire. The Ottomans controlled Bosphorus, a waterway and this led to the war of the Crusades. The Christians were upset that they could not have access to Jerusalem, the Holy City. The European Christians were then forced to find a different sea route to India and Asia. This lead to the discovery of America.

Dr. Bennett explained that the Ottoman Empire was Balkanised (split into many countries) during World War 1. He asked us to watch the movie 'Lawrence of Arabia', which I later saw. Turkey was now neither a part of Europe nor accepted by Asia. The whole book is set against this backdrop.

The story is about a doctor, Dr. Sennahadin, his wife, his children and his grandchildren. Turkey was undergoing a metamorphosis under Kemal Pasha Attaturk (Father of Turkey). It was getting Westernised and religion was taking a backseat. Fez caps and burkas were banned. Women were given the right to vote. Turks frequented bars. Communism and nationalism spread across the country. The Hegira calendar was changed to Gregorian calendar. Dr. Bennett mentioned that the Turks are melancholic because of the loss of identity. He also mentions that a history is for slaves and we should not disturb them. The future is for us. Dr. Bennett mentioned that this book is episodic (like a TV serial) and not linear.

Later on, the audience discussed about Russia, Arabs, Lebanon, Kuwait, Saddam Hussain, Persians, Anti-Semitic, Aryans, Kurds, even Sofia Museum and the Coptic Christians of Egypt. I did not understand much of the story but it was a great experience.

'Not Just An Accountant' by Vinod Rai (CAG):

On March 23rd, 2016, I got an opportunity to attend another book club meeting with my mom. This time, Mr. Gopalakrishnan, Former Executive Director of BHEL, reviewed the book 'Not Just an Accountant - The Diary of the Nation's Conscience Keeper' by Mr. Vinod Rai, the former Comptroller Auditor General (CAG). As it was a book related to politics, finance and economics, I had to do some homework before going to the meeting. I sat down with my mom and checked out the contents of the book on the internet.

Mr. Gopalakrishnan reviewed the book in four parts. Part one was about the experiences of a CAG. Part two was about the types of audits which take place. Part three and four were about media policy and CBI and their roles.

This book is a series of documented evidence about the various issues and scams in the 1990s. The highlight and eagerly awaited part of the review was about the Coalgate and 2G scams. I was shocked to note that an exorbitant amount of money was swindled at the highest level. The book stated that there is a 12 fold increase in the net worth of billionaires in India. Mr. Gopalakrishnan also talked about the 'jugaad mechanism' of Indians.

Finally, he finished on a positive note saying that Indians can still be appreciated for being adaptable and solution oriented. For this, he gave two examples. In 1967, when the Arab War was happening and the stock markets in India were crashing, the people of Kerala and Tamil Nadu started looking for other options.

They sought for jobs in Saudi Arabia. They started earning and sent a lot of foreign exchange back to India.

The second example was that of M. S. Swaminathan who is known as the Father of the Green Revolution in India. When he introduced a programme under which high yield varieties of wheat and rice were planted in the fields of poor Indian farmers, these poor people adapted to the change immediately and very easily. With this, the entire review ended on a positive note. After the meeting I spoke to Mr. Gopalakrishnan and also took a photo with him.

Pragyan-The Tech Festival at NIT, Trichy

It is an annual event conducted by the students of NIT, Trichy. Here, I attended a few talks and wish to share excerpts from two talks which impressed me.

Dr. Abhas Mitra (Astrophysicist)

Dr. Mitra said that X-rays and gamma rays don't transmit complete information from the stars but gravitational waves do. He explained how gravitational waves were detected by LIGO. He shared a very interesting concept about negative mass. It is a hypothetical concept of matter which is the opposite of mass, eg. -5kg. It is used in speculative theories like wormholes.

Dr. Archana Sharma (CERN, physicist)

Dr. Archana is a physicist from BHU (Banaras Hindu University) and the only Indian working with CERN, Switzerland since 1987. She works with colliders which are 27 kilometres long. They need 20 million amps of current, 10 tesla magnetic field, 500 tonnes of liquefied Helium and have to maintain temperatures of 1.8 Kelvin.

She gave a beautiful explanation for Higgs Boson-the God particle.

She said imagine a room full of people walking aimlessly and randomly. All of a sudden Rajinikanth enters the room. He would be the centre of attention. People would rush to be around him. Similarly, Higgs Boson is the "Rajinikanth particle". Those closer to him i.e protons and neutrons would be heavier, those further away i.e electrons would be lighter.

I saw a lot of exhibits too. I saw a robot which had 500 movements and touch sensors. I witnessed an automated chessboard and also a 3D printer but unfortunately, could not see a live demonstration. I saw a concrete block with ferrous carbonate which would absorb carbondioxide and reduce global warming and have greater strength. I had fun playing soccer with a robot and operated a flight simulator. Overall, it was an enthralling experience.

Yi (Young Indians) Seminar

Yi was formed in 2002 and is an integral part of Confederation of Indian Industry (CII). It is a non-government, not for profit industry led and industry managed organization. The Yi includes the young members between the age group of 21 and 40.

I attended one Yi conference on January 22 and 23 in Trichy at Hotel Sangam. I was thrilled to note that a company from Trichy is a supplier of roasted nuts to Walmart. There was a presentation by many would-be start-ups. Thanks to the exposure, I could understand what they said. I was also a very active participant in the seminar. One of the most interesting stories was that of 'Happy Hens'. This company is run by Mr. Ashok Kannan who is a paraplegic. I was informed that broiler hens are the prime reason of cancer and depression. The problem to this solution was free and happy hens. The entrepreneur was working on selling organic eggs to the USA and scaling up the operation. I was pleased to note that there is a start-up club in Trichy.

During the lunch break, I met many entrepreneurs. I interacted with Mr. Shankar Narayanan, the co-founder of Nexus.Inc. He shared with me many tips on how I could start my own business. I also interacted with Dr. Velumani, the chairman of Thyrocare, the national leader in medical diagnostic business. He asked me what I wanted to become, I confidently told him that I wanted to do everything. He suggested that instead of saying everything, I should say anything. I asked him what was the difference,

Dr. Velumani said, "When you say everything you lose focus, when you say anything, you have confidence and focus." This was the best advice I received in my USY.

The most fascinating talk was given by Mr. Sujith Kumar of Infosys. I took in every word of what he said just like a butterfly takes to nectar. He told the story of an Olympic swimming champion and of cricketer, Marcus Trescothick. Both of them did not like the sport they had chosen. What made them excel was practice, practice and practice. Mr. Sujith even cited the example of Rahul Dravid, who was humble enough to take advice from a 19-year-old on how to improve his game.

Mr. Sujith told about the transformation process in his son. His son would only part with his old toys. On seeing the plight of a family which was affected by Chennai floods, his son gave away his brand new cricket bat to a child of that family. Mr. Sujith was proud to see this transformation in his son. His son also organised a programme for the exchange gifts between his school which is private and a government-run school.

Mr. Sujith shared a striking story of a poor boy who turned into an entrepreneur. This poor boy used to go from house to house and run errands. Once Mr. Sujith gave him a business idea. He mentioned that there were some flat owners in their area who had dogs. As the owners were extremely busy, they could not take their dogs for exercise. Hence, the dogs were becoming obese and having health problems. Mr. Sujith asked the poor lad to charge a small fee for exercising these dogs. A few years later, Mr. Sujith was standing on the roadside. A car stopped next to him and the window rolled down. The person inside said, "Sir, do you recognise me? I am that poor boy. Today I have 60 employees working under me. I have a contract throughout Chennai for taking dogs for a walk. It was all your idea and I wish to thank you. Please visit my website." Mr. Sujith also spoke about how his passion made him start Maatran Foundation, a tie-up between Infosys and many colleges. The colleges offer 100 percent scholarship to deserving students and Mr. Sujith handpicks these students. He paraphrased a quote of Paul Coelho, "If your intention is right, universe will support you."

Toastmasters International (TI)

This is a International Club spread across 135 countries and has over 15,000 clubs attached to it. The aim of the club is to improve the public speaking skills of its members.

Last year (2015) in the month of October, I got an opportunity to attend the Division Contest of TI called 'Sangamam'. It happened at Abdur Rehman University, Chennai. A Humorous speech and Table Topics Contest took place here. The participants were from Chennai, Trichy, Madurai & Virudhnagar. Participants who had won speech competitions at their Club level & Area level contested here.

My mother was also one of the participants and I was proud of it. My dad had come third in a similar competition held in 2014. Though, at that time I didn't have a clear idea about Toastmasters, I thoroughly enjoyed the sessions and got to meet many distinguished Toastmasters like TM Nina John, TM Sastharam and TM Pravin Mani. The only disappointment for me was that my mother could not win in the competition, but that's part of the game.

Next, I got a chance to attend one more Division Contest called 'Dimension' in the month of April 2016 at NIT- Trichy. My parents belong to the Trichy Toastmasters Club. This was the first time that a Division Contest was happening in Trichy and the Trichy Toastmasters Club was the host. There was a speech competition yet again. The entire atmosphere was filled with excitement and learning. For me the memorable part of the conference was meeting Mr. P C Bala, a well known author and speaker. He was invited to deliver a guest lecture to the audience. I thoroughly enjoyed his talk, which was from his well known book "Rajini's Punchtantra". Bala uncle was able to keep the audience engaged by connecting certain Management mantras with popular dialogues from 'Superstar' Rajinikant's movies. As usual, I didn't lose the opportunity of meeting Bala uncle and taking a snap with him.

My recent stint with Toastmasters was in Chennai in the month of May 2016. I accompanied my parents to the Toastmasters International conference called the 'Ovation'. I learnt that there were many International participants in this conference. The entire program was organised on a massive scale in Mahindra City – Chennai.

I was thrilled because we were going to stay in a star hotel called 'Holiday Inn', but was disappointed with the poor service. We arrived at 11pm and were starving. My mom ordered for some burgers and hot chocolate. It took the room service nearly thirty minutes to tell us that burgers were not available. Finally after several calls we got some sandwiches and hot chocolate by midnight. The frustrating part was that the hot chocolate was prepared from burnt milk. I was really surprised that such things could happen in a star hotel.

Next morning we went into the sprawling campus of "Infosys" to attend the conference. The ambience, the food and all the arrangements were perfect. I got a chance to meet many toastmasters from different clubs, International speakers and guests from different walks of life. Some of my memorable moments at this conference were as follows:

Meeting author and speaker Barbara Khozam from USA; I was immediately captivated by her smile and towering personality. She was extremely warm and friendly. Barbara has written a book called 'How organisations deliver bad customer service'. She was one of the guest speakers at the conference and spoke on the topic of 'Body Language'. I learnt many points from her speech. The best part was when I volunteered to be on stage and she demonstrated to the audience on different types of handshakes.

Barbara shared a very moving experience. She had divorced and was going through a traumatic period. It was Toastmasters which helped her overcome the battle in her mind and become a successful motivational speaker. She was truly inspiring. Later I spoke to her in person and told her that I was on the verge of completing a book. Barbara gave me many tips on how to publish and promote the book .

A week before attending the conference, I had seen an interview of Mr. C.K.Kumaravel, the CEO of Naturals (India's largest chain of beauty parlours) on the You Tube I had already done a project at Naturals. Now seeing him in person gave me goose bumps. It was beyond the wildest of my dreams.

Mr. Kumaravel mainly addressed on the importance of 'Women Entrepreneurship'. He shared many interesting anecdotes to explain his points. The line which I liked the most was – 'Your dream is your signature and let the whole world know it'. Mr. Kumaravel shared about a lady from Karur (a town near Trichy) who is from a rich family but wanted to be more independent. She took up the franchise of 'Naturals' and now earns more than Rs 50,000 a month. When Mr. Kumaravel asked her why she wanted to run a business of her own in spite of being wealthy, she replied that she wanted independence in making her own decisions. I wish every woman in India could be independent like her.

The minute Mr. Kumaravel finished his speech; I jumped out of my seat and ran to meet him. As always, I asked him to pose for a photo with me. What happened next took me by surprise. Mr. Kumaravel, took out his phone and clicked a selfie with me! This was a memorable moment for me.

I wish to mention about Mr.Sastharam, who I admire very much. He is one of the youngest District Governors in the Toastmasters fraternity. I have always seen him bubbly, friendly and ever smiling. He narrated how the entire toastmasters community in and around Chennai came together to rescue the flood affected people.

On the whole, I enjoyed the experience. The speech contest was captivating. I heard some amazing speeches. The most memorable among them were by TM Shyam Raj from Virudhunagar and TM Kaishika Rodrigo from Colombo. I wish to become a Toastmaster soon.

Attending seminars has increased my thirst for knowledge even more.

Notes from the parents:

Sagarikka constantly keeps asking us what she should become in life. We always tell her that it is for her to decide. This is a very difficult decision for us, as in our town, it is the parent who decides the destiny of the child. But until now, we have been telling our kid, that it is upto her to decide.

We repeatedly go through the lines of 'Khalil Gibran' – *your children are not your children, they are the sons and daughters of life longing for themselves. Though they are with you, they do not belong to you. Give them your love, but not your thoughts, for they have their own thoughts.* These few lines prevent us from resorting to our temptation of telling her what to do.

We also read a lot of literature on the 'Law of Attraction', which states that - *every child is manifested into this world for a specific purpose. Each child operates at a particular frequency. The duty of the parent is not to interfere with this frequency. When the child is given adequate space and time, she will resonate and fulfil her purpose.*

This has been the most difficult decision for us to make. At times, we feel that we know what is best for our child but we keep our mouth shut.

PERSONAL EXPERIENCE

- OUT OF THE BOX
- READING MAKETH A WO(MAN)
- EDUCATION: THE BEDROCK OF LIFE
- HEALTH IS WEALTH
- INTO THE WORLD OF COMPUTING
- UNDERSTANDING LIFE

OUT OF THE BOX

Blogging

At the start of my USY, I met Mr. Siddhartha Joshi, a Punekar and a traveller. His passion is to discover people's dreams and he is a regular blogger on this subject. He is the prime reason why I got into blogging.

Right from the beginning of my USY I started recording all my activities. This led me to blogging. I guessed that if 50 people read my blogs, it would be great. I wrote my first blog and asked the Mr. & Mrs. Architect of my life to correct the grammatical errors. I posted it the next day. The reviews gave me a mild heart attack. There were more than 500 views. The more I wrote, the more my confidence grew. I had never in my wildest of dreams guessed that I would one day become a writer. As they say "The journey of a thousand miles starts with the first step". A few months into blogging, wherever I went, seminars or meetings, people would ask me, "Have you started writing your next blog?" I would say, "Yes! I will post it tomorrow." Most of the time, I forgot to do so!

Creating advertisement

My parents have been running a Coaching Institute for the last 18 years. I suggested that they advertise their products on television to generate more revenue. Finally, I took the initiative.

My intuition was that black and white advertisement would appeal to the audience. My guess was that people see only colour on TV and black and white would stand out. But what kind of black and white ad should I make? I chose stop motion and I downloaded an application. I posted a series of pictures in this app. I merged sounds along with these pictures. The whole process took me a couple of hours. I felt that the ad was brilliant. Mr. Naveen S Kumar, an architecture student and a short film maker, gave the final touches. My parents did not take any initiative to release the ad in the local television channels. I later uploaded it on YouTube, but got very few views. It was disheartening.

Documentary

Before my trip to Mount Kailash, my parents suggested that I make a documentary on my return. I had no idea on how to make one, but I accepted the challenge. During my trip, I clicked pictures and took videos. Many a time I forgot about the documentary. The trip was fun, but dad constantly kept reminding me and literally goaded me into taking pictures. On my return to Trichy, I went to Voicecare Studio to do the recording. Vijay uncle (owner of the studio), was very helpful. He gave me a hefty discount and made my documentary in record time. I posted it on YouTube, thinking, it would become a blockbuster, but many people could not view it. It was either because of the size of my video or because I copied the background music from Chevaliers de Sangreal. I later uploaded the same video in a low quality version. I waited for a couple of days. There were 500 views.

I was better planned on my next tour to Leh. I was now experienced in the art of documentary making. I was assisted by Ms. Hetal, my friend who had a DSLR camera. We took great pictures of scenic views. I now knew how to make a documentary on my own. Once again with the help of Mr. Naveen S Kumar, I completed this project within a week.

I expected more views, but this one got lesser views than the Mount Kailash documentary.

This video had actually come out much better than the Kailash video. For the Kailash documentary, 10 percent of the pictures were taken by me and 90 percent were downloaded from Google. For the Leh documentary, it was the other way around. To this day, I am amused, why originality was not appreciated.

Notes from the parents:

We attended a training programme called Landmark. The trainer asked us to imagine a red car in a room that was brightly lit with yellow light. He asked us, what would be the colour of the 'red car'. Then he answered that it would be 'yellow'. No matter how much we polish the car, it would still be yellow.

The trainer cited another example. He said that children are spirits, but like the genie of Alladin, they are 'Bottled' by the education system.

We took this example to heart. We then decided to break the bottle and let the genie in Pappu out. We would let her out of the 'yellow' lit room, so that she could enjoy her *own essence*. This would then allow her to be herself, before she stepped back into the 'yellow' lit room.

We were constantly plagued by doubts and apprehensions.

However, once we resolved there was no turning back. We had to take complete responsibility for the USY project.

READING MAKETH A WO(MAN)

My cousin lives in Bengaluru and is two years younger to me. Whenever I meet him, he is into some book; Isaac Asimov, 'Hardy Boys', 'Harry Potter' series, Sherlock Holmes or even Arthur C. Clarke. I used to have a severe complex meeting him but I never got myself into reading books. In my school, we preferred to discuss about movies and TV serials, but books were a big NO. My parents' only regret is that they did not develop my reading habit when I was young.

During my USY project, my father made it his mission to make me read books. Whether we were in the car, hotel lounge, at a marriage function or even in a park, he would make me read out from a book and ask me to explain every line of it. It was very embarrassing as strangers and onlookers would stare at us. Some of them would even stand by the side and watch what was happening. I found it very funny and would become self-conscious. Dad would provoke me to proceed regardless of the fact that people were watching. Following are some of the books I got to read in my USY.

The High Performing Entrepreneur (By Subroto Bagchi)

Mr. Subroto Bagchi has written a superb book. I understood the meaning of writing a business plan, DNA, mission, vision and values. I understood terms like choosing the right investor, process focused organisation and building the brand. I was also inspired by the many examples given by Mr. Bagchi.

Mr. Bagchi sold balloons when he was six years old. He said that choosing the balloon, breathing air into it, tying it up with a string and giving a sales talk is value addition. I understood that nothing should be given free and I should charge for whatever service I provide including selling of products because it is value addition.

Mr. Bagchi mentions that Mr. Azim Premji of Wipro works 80 hours a week. There is a great quote in the book of Vikram Seth, "Long distance runners go through segmented pain." I have to go a long way in life and I have to put in a lot of hard work and segment my pain.

There are two incidents written in the book that had a deep impact on me.

There was a gentleman working with Mr. Bagchi, who wanted to start a business of his own. He convinced two of his colleagues to join him for the venture. Before starting his new venture, he met Mr. Bagchi in his cabin leaving his colleagues outside the room. He asked him, whether he could join the company back if this new business of his failed. Mr. Bagchi says in his book that this gentleman is bound to fail because he is looking at failure as an option. An entrepreneur should never see failure as an option. This gentleman also lacked integrity because he was prepared to ditch two of his colleagues who were willing to sacrifice their jobs and go with him.

The other story was about Mr. Siddharth of Cafe Coffee Day fame whose family was in the coffee estate business. This business was not profitable as the price of coffee kept fluctuating as per demand. Mr. Siddharth observed that though coffee growers were having a tough time, the person selling a cup of coffee could quote the price he wanted. Mr. Siddharth hit upon a brilliant idea. Why not take control of the entire coffee chain? Be the grower and the seller. He started purchasing acres of coffee estate. He would manufacture the coffee and sell the beverage at the price he desired. Thus, the whole profit would go to him.

This book also taught me to respect Goddess Lakshmi. This goddess is very possessive and would walk out of the house, where she is not given importance. Mr. Bagchi says don't say "I don't want money", Goddess Lakshmi could be listening and walk out of the house forever.

I wish to thank Mr. Rostow Ravanan for his words of advice in this book in the chapter "Idea to IPO". I shall implement his suggestions while buying shares.

Once again I would like to thank Bagchi uncle for this wonderful book. I made a PowerPoint presentation of this book for my parent's staff. This book is a must read for every entrepreneur.

Eat that Frog (By Brian Tracy)

This was the second book that I read. It is a very interesting book on goal setting. Frog, according to Mr. Brian Tracy, is the most important task on which we procrastinate. This book mentions a beautiful quote by Mark Twain. It says, "Each morning if you eat a live frog, you can go through the day with a satisfaction of knowing that it is the worst thing that can happen to you all day long." Mr. Tracy asks a question, "How do you eat an elephant?" The answer is - one bite at a time!

He gives an awesome example for this in the chapter 'Take It One Barrel at a Time'. The Sahara Desert is 500 miles long. There is no water, food or even a blade of grass on this stretch. Nobody could construct a road as sand would cover it. Many travellers had got lost in the desert and more than 1,300 people had died while crossing it.

A French man then got a great idea. He placed 55 gallon oil drums every five kilometres across the desert. Why five kilometres? This is because the earth curves every five kilometres and this is the distance to the horizon. As soon as the traveller reached a barrel, he could see a barrel at the horizon. When he reached the next barrel, he could see the very next barrel and so on. So taking one step at a time, even the great Sahara can be crossed. Mr. Tracy says that even a big task can be accomplished by placing barrels at regular distances. This example had a big impact on me.

I learnt terms like KRA, 10 to 90 percent rule and Pareto Principle.

Mr. Tracy shared a thought provoking quote of Goethe, "Things that matter the most should not be at the mercy of things that matter the least" Mr. Tracy said that technology can be your best friend and worst enemy. I made a decision to reduce my Whatsapp interaction, Facebook viewing and chatting. I profusely thank Mr. Tracy for this advice.

The chapter 'Use ABCDE Method Continually' was the icing on the cake. The ABCDE Method is a priority-setting technique. A stands for must do. B stands for should do. C stands for nice to do. D stands for delegate to someone else and E stands for eliminate. My school starts soon and I am putting all my energy into writing the book 'My USY' because my priorities will shift.

Positioning (By Al Ries and Jack Trout)

I had no idea about marketing. In the beginning of my USY, my dad took me to the Nilgiris supermarket in the neighbourhood. The staff there were very friendly. They explained to me about all products. They told me about inventory, reorder quantity, shelf space and Point of Purchase. They explained that children's products like biscuits and chocolates are displayed in the lower shelf as children were of lesser height and would be able to see the products only at that level. It was here that I understood that Rin, Wheel, Pepsodent and Lux are from Hindustan Lever; Gillette, Ariel and Pampers are from Proctor and Gamble; Maggie, Kit Kat and Nescafe are from Nestle.

My dad's next project was to make me read the book 'Positioning.' The authors asked a question, "Who was the first man to cross the Atlantic?" Charles Lindbergh. Who were the second and third? Nobody cares; nobody bothers. A major learning from the book is "Positioning is not what you do to the product; it is what you do to the minds of the people." Marketing is a game played in the six inch grey matter between the ears. The author states that you should be the first to enter the market (mind space) like Charles Lindbergh. If you are the second, then follow Amelia Earhart strategy. Amelia Earhart crossed the Atlantic after many men had crossed it, but we remember her because she was the first woman to do so.

The book is replete with examples. There is a chapter on the strategy a market leader should follow. The author gives the example of Gillette which has multiple brands; Gillette, Trac II, Atra, Good News!, Sensor, Mach 3. This is the reason why competitors find it difficult to create a niche in the razor market. Gillette knew how to cover all bets. Crest toothpaste made the mistake of not doing so and lost its leadership to Colgate.

The book shares a very interesting example of why America is named after Amerigo Vespucci. Though Christopher Columbus was the first one to reach its shores, he made the mistake of looking for gold and keeping his mouth shut. Amerigo Vespucci didn't. He positioned the new world as a separate continent, totally distinct from Asia. He wrote extensively of his discoveries and theories. This mistake of Columbus was the reason why he lost a great chance of having two continents named after him.

The book suggests that you should always look for a hole (Cherchez le creneaux). Would anyone buy a short, fat and ugly car? Yes, people did. Volkswagen Beetle proved to be a big success. The rationale; all cars in those days were long, lean and beautiful. People wanted something different. That is why Volkswagen Beetle was a mega success.

The book talks about the positioning of Belgium. Though Belgium is a beautiful country, nobody says that he is going to Belgium for a holiday. Why not? When we say England we think of the Big Ben and Tower of London. When we say Amsterdam we think of tulips and Rembrandt. When we say France, we think of Louvre and Eiffel Tower, but when we say Belgium we think of '...'

The authors state that Sabena (Belgium airline) is one of the best airlines in the world, but is not famous, because it is in the wrong country.

I made a PowerPoint presentation for the staff about this book also.

Dr. Abdul Kalam, Dr. C. V. Raman, writer Sujatha and actor Sivakarthikeyan are all from Trichy. Had they continued living in Trichy, they would have become another Sabena. They became famous because they left Trichy. One thing I understand from this book is that my success doesn't depend only on hard work; it also depends on the horse I ride on.

The book has only case studies of American products. I wish there was a book with Indian examples. I also wish that our supermarkets are filled with Indian brands. With so many brilliant engineers and scientists in this country, can't we make razor blades, world-class soaps, toothpastes and detergents?

Blue Ocean Strategy (By Chan Kim and Renee Mauborgne)

At a Young Indians conference in Trichy, I met Mr. Gowrishankar. He is a Blue Ocean Strategist and works with Chan Kim. He is working on a project of creating a Blue Ocean Strategy in Malaysian jails where the criminals were made to work in Army camps. This reduced recidivism (returning to crime).

Mr. Gowrishankar shared numerous examples. He mentioned that Roentgen invented the X-ray but GE made the money. SEGWAY is a self-balancing electric vehicle for personal transportation. The manufacturer expected it to be a game changer but it failed on the price point. He also spoke about why Google glass is a failure.

I learnt two interesting things. One, Microsoft never needs a new product. Visual Basic, C++, MSM, SKYPE and even Excel were all bought from software developers, packaged and marketed. Finally, there was an Indian example. Mr. Gowrishankar spoke about the Chik shampoo. Mr. Ranganathan, the founder of Cavin Kare (the manufacturer of Chik shampoo) would send his team to various villages with shampoo sachets. His team would visit schools and offer the children trial packs. The children loved the product giving the parents no other option but to buy the shampoo. Thus, Chik became a more popular brand than the other well-known brands in Hindustan Unilever.

You can guess what happened next. Now I wanted to read the book 'Blue Ocean Strategy.' I found the book very similar to Positioning. The book states that there are two oceans - The Red Ocean, where there is extensive competition and The Blue Ocean, where there is no competition. The author suggests that to enter the blue ocean, one should create a strategy canvas. In this canvas, the current strategy of the competitors should be drawn. Some of the factors should be reduced or eliminated and some raised or created.

I enjoyed reading the case study of Yellow-Tail Wines. An Australian company, Casella Wines discovered a blue ocean. It made a boring and a complicated drink like wine; fun, adventurous. Cirque du Soleil was a compelling story. I thought that circus is a place of star performers, animal shows, fun and humour, thrills and danger. Cirque du Soleil removed all these factors. How could a circus survive without these elements? Cirque du Soleil instead introduced themes, multiple productions, music and dance. It became a big hit and the best part of it was, they also increased the price.

I also liked the story of Novo Nordisk. This company discovered that the insulin supplied in vials, to diabetics, was very difficult to administer. Patients had to handle syringes and needles and administer the doses according to their needs. Needles and syringes also created unpleasant feelings in patients. They did not want others to see them when they were injecting themselves. Novo Nordisk solved this problem by creating NovoPen. This resembled a fountain pen and contained a week's worth of insulin. The patient just had to click the pen to inject himself. This created a Blue Ocean for Novo Nordisk. Today, it has a big market share worldwide.

The best story was that of Cemex, a cement manufacturer in Mexico. This company made a boring product like cement; emotional. End result, today people in Mexico offer Cemex cement as a token of love at wedding functions. This cement would help the newlyweds construct their own house and thereby fulfil their dreams. What a Blue Ocean!

The book lists out a step-by-step plan to create a Blue Ocean. I went through the four steps of visualising strategy. I then made a presentation to my parents on how I was going to enter the blue oceans in my upcoming projects.

How I Raised Myself from Failure to SUCCESS IN SELLING (By Frank Bettger)

This was the easiest book for me to read during my USY. This book was first published in 1951 and I found it very useful during my selling experience. There are three anecdotes in it that I want to share with you in particular.

There was a strong man in a nightclub. He allowed the audience to hit him in the stomach as hard as they could. Many men tried but this man was unfazed. One night a Swede came to the club, who did not understand English. Instead of hitting the strong man in the stomach, the Swede hit him on the jaw and knocked him out. Moral of the story: Pick up the most vulnerable point in the customer and focus all your energy on that. Mr. Bettger explained this method through another story. He wanted to buy a house and met a real estate agent who kept on asking questions till he found out that Mr. Bettger wanted to have a tree in the house. He took him to a far off place and showed a house surrounded by trees. Mr. Bettger asked for the price of the house. The agent quoted a very high price. He objected but the agent kept on talking about the trees knowing very well that it was Mr. Bettger's weakness. Finally, the house was sold to him.

This book has many techniques on how to ask the customers the right questions, the why technique and the '*in addition to*' technique! I used these techniques during my selling experience and found them effective.

The next anecdote which left a mark on me was about the period when Railways became the new mode of transport and wanted to build a bridge.

The steamboat companies got worried that they would lose their business. They got a stay order from the court. This resulted in a big lawsuit. The steamboat owners hired a lawyer called Wead, who gave his final talk in the court for two hours. The audience was spellbound and gave a loud applause. The railroad lawyer was a poorly dressed, long, lanky, obscure fellow. His closing speech lasted for only a minute. He said, "The only question for you to decide is whether a man has more right to travel up and down the river, than he has to cross the river." Then the jury came to the conclusion that the Railways was right. The poorly dressed lawyer won the case. He was none other than Abraham Lincoln. What I learnt from this anecdote was, what can be said in one sentence need not be explained for hours.

The final anecdote was how Mr. Bettger got inspired by Benjamin Franklin and made a 3" × 5" card as a pocket reminder. The card list was as follows:

Enthusiasm
Order: self-organisation
Think in terms of others' interest
Questions
Key issue
Silence: listen
Sincerity: deserve confidence
Knowledge of my business
Appreciation and praise
Smile: happiness
Remember names and faces
Service and prospecting
Closing the sale: action

The first week Mr. Bettger would concentrate only on enthusiasm. The next week he would only concentrate on order: self-organisation. He would proceed in the same manner every week. Each week, he gained a clearer understanding of the topic deep inside himself. His business became more interesting and exciting.

At the end of 13 weeks, he would go back to the beginning of his list. This made him stronger and stronger in all the points. Though I like the idea, I have not made a list so far. I plan to do it in future.

Follow Every Rainbow (By Rashmi Bansal)

It is a book about 25 enterprising woman who raised family as well as company. These are women from different backgrounds but with one single dream - To make a mark in the world of business.

There are three stories from this book that inspire me a lot. I would like to share them with you:-

Patricia Narayanan - Caterer

Patricia Narayanan was born in Nagercoil. In 1977, she fell in love with a caterer who worked opposite to her college. He was a Hindu while she was a Christian. After marriage, she came to know that he was an alcoholic. She was a college dropout and had no job. Initially, she made artificial flowers and supplied to hotels as she had no money. Many a time, she felt like committing suicide. After a long struggle, she got the permission to set up a snack stall on the Marina Beach called Clarke Snack Bar. She earned 50 paisa from her first sales. Slowly, her stall became a popular hangout for people. The Walkers Association on Marina Beach gave her an opportunity to cater for a programme and she took the opportunity and was successful. She never compromised on the quality of the food. If something went wrong, she would throw the food away and cook it again. Within a few years, she got many contracts and employed more than 70 people. Later, she got a divorce and in 1996, she started with her own restaurant called Chef Susan. She started the restaurant in her daughter's name which has 12 to 13 units now in Chennai with over 200 employees. In January 2012, she got the 'Women Entrepreneur of the Year' award from FICCI. She also started a charitable ambulance service in the area where her daughter died due to an accident.

Jasumathi Ashra – Sculptor

Jasumathi Ashra was from a well-to-do business family. When she was 13 years old, she painted a six-feet high canvas for her school exhibition and won a cash price of Rs.500. Mrs. Jasumathi went on a study tour to Gwalior from college. There she saw a statue of the Rani of Jhansi and got inspired by it. Later, she met her future husband and her family disowned her. She took the surname 'Shilpi' and her name became Jasu Shilpi. Both were teachers and had no money, thus society didn't respect them. So she decided to become rich. In 1975, the Municipal Corporation of Rajkot floated a tender for a statue. Not to miss this opportunity, Mrs. Jasu met the mayor. Though she had no experience, she had very good communication skills and got the tender. They paid her Rs.25,000 to make the statue of Dr. B. R. Ambedkar. She got help from an artist in Bangladesh for this. In a short period of time, she made the statue successfully. With the little money they had, they set a livelihood for themselves. In due course of time, her husband passed away. But her resilience pushed her back to her vocation. Her dream was to make a statue of Sivaji and she was the first woman to do it. Her inspiration to make the statue of Rani of Jhansi's became a reality too. She also got the order for a Gandhi statue from the US and Hanuman statue from Rajasthan. She says that sculpting could fetch anywhere between 16 lakh to 1.2 crore per statue and the cost involved is only for the bronze, artist skill and labourers. Her advice to all women is when a woman has to achieve something, she has to be ready to sacrifice her routine life.

Dipali Sikand – Les Concierges

After completing her ninth standard, she worked in a travel agency. During tenth, she went to the Himalayan Mountaineering Institute and was trained under Tenzing Norgay. That time, she also went till the base camp of Mount Everest. Dipali was the student union leader in her college and also the Youth Congress leader in Delhi. As she had bitter experiences with politicians, she left her post. She joined ESSAR as an HR manager. Since she had a challenging personal life, she fought back to get her freedom. Mrs. Dipali started Les Concierges (providing services and solutions) and her first order was from iGate and gradually, she also got orders from Wipro and other companies. By the end of first year, her company had 140 employees and by 2004, her annual revenue was three crore. They introduced a new product called Ms. Moneypenny – the perfect receptionist. Mrs. Dipali even started international forays in 2008. She had 1300 offices by 2011 and her revenue was 56 crores. Over 40 percent to 45 percent orders were from the IT sector. 75 percent of her staff was only female. In 2006, she got married again to Rajeev, a musician and started Kyra a theatre-cum-restaurant in Bengaluru.

These six books have given me a deep insight into life. Mr. Bagchi would never have the time to meet me and teach me business, but he spoke to me through the book. Attending one seminar of Mr. Tracy would cost thousands of rupees, but I was able to get the essence of his teachings from his book. Marketing gurus Al Ries and Chan Kim shared the secrets of marketing through their book. Mr. Frank Bettger, the greatest salesmen ever, can no longer teach me as he is no more. Thanks to Ms. Rashmi Bansal's efforts, I was able to get the complete experience of 25 leading women entrepreneurs.

The books I want to read next are - *My Experiments with Truth* by Mahatma Gandhi, *Long Walk to Freedom* by Nelson Mandela, Amish Tripathi's *The Shiva Trilogy*, Books on Creativity by Edward de Bono and Warren Buffet's books on investing

Notes from the parents:

Savitri and I have been voracious readers. We chose not to have a television in our house for many years. People would never believe us when we told them that. We have a huge collection of books. The popular Tamil magazine 'Aanantha Vikatan' discovered this fact and devoted an entire article to our book collection on the World Book Day.

Whenever we sat down to read, Pappu would vanish from the scene. She preferred to go out and play with her friends. To her, sitting in one place and reading a book was a mundane activity. Being a kinaesthetic child, she prefered to move around

We regret the mistake to this day. We should have disciplined her and *made her read or read out to her* for at least 15 minutes everyday.

Once we heard a TED Talk about the importance of books. The speaker said – when I want spiritual advice, I go to Dalai Lama. When I want scientific advice, I go to Richard Feynman. When I want investment advice, I go to Warren Buffet. For political advice, it is Nelson Mandela. For body building, I seek the advice of Arnold Schwarzenegger. They all live in my house… in my library.

To make amends, we started on a mission to zealously make Pappu read. It was half an hour of newspaper in the mornings and 45 minutes of *book reading*, late in the evenings.

EDUCATION: THE BEDROCK OF LIFE

My teacher labelled me as an attention deficit, hyperactive child. My parents would be periodically called to school. The regular complaint was that I was not paying attention in class. I would keep looking out of the window. The teachers were right. Even during exams, I found it difficult to sit through two-and-a half hours and complete a paper. I would repeatedly drop my pencil and rubber, so that I could get beneath the desk. I would sit there and spend some time. In my middle school, I was given permission to come out of the class. I would sit on the swing and spend time on the slide for hours. The only reason I went to school was because I had a lot of friends. I enjoyed my lunch breaks where we would share our lunch. The Physical Training period was the best part of the day.

I found my tenth standard Mathematics very challenging. The whole chapter on Polynomials was Greek and Latin to me. I could not make head or tail out of Factorisation and Remainder Theorem. I kept wondering why there was a subject called Geometry, it was full of axioms and theorems. Every week, there was a test. I was going from one test to another with no idea what it all meant. Science was better but I was uncomfortable with electricity and the chapter on carbon and its compounds. I could visualise and understand some of the concepts in Science. This made me feel at ease in the Science class.

I totally detested the Social Science period. I had no clue about the Indian Constitution or the Indian Economy. I used to wonder why I had to learn by- heart the history of Cambodia or the government structure of Belgium. I did not even know about the history and the government of India. What was Prussia doing in Germany? What was the difference between civil disobedience movement and non-cooperation movement? Why did Garibaldi help King Victor Emmanuel-II of Sardinia-Piedmont to pull on the boot named Italy? I felt like Ishaan Awasti from Taare Zameen Par. Everything was spinning around me. I presumed that my classmates were more intelligent than I was; they seemed to understand subjects better.

Fortunately it was USY that saved me. But for it, I would have been dumb. In the beginning of my USY, I needed a lot of confidence and motivation from my parents to understand the importance of different subjects. It was taking me time to connect the dots.

I connected very well with the story of Thomas Alva Edison. Edison's school teacher wrote to his mother that Edison was addled and wouldn't be allowed in school anymore. When Edison asked his mother what the letter was about, she read out the contents of it loudly to him – "Your son is a genius. This school is too small for him and doesn't have good teachers to teach him. Please teach him yourself."

Many years after Edison's mother died, he saw a folded paper in the corner of a drawer. He opened it up and saw what was written. It was the letter that the school teacher had written to his mother. Edison cried for hours and later wrote in his diary, "An addled child of a heroic mother became the genius of the century." His mother protected his self-image so that he could rise to his fullest potential. I perceived that my parents were doing the same. They were protecting my self-image.

During my USY, I used to devote 6 to 9 pm to Maths and Physics every day and 9 to 9.45 pm for reading books. Every morning was committed to reading newspapers and building my vocabulary. Saturdays and Sundays were spent solving CAT and SAT papers. My evening routine was a constant one except for Saturday evenings when we would go for a family outing. Even at Mount Kailash, we spent some time doing Maths and Science.

Slowly, I started discovering the underlying magic of Mathematics. I was made to do my entire Geometry on graph paper. Geometry was no longer scary. It was a beautiful pattern which I had mistaken for some meaningless theorems. I was then made to draw the entire concept of linear equalities on graph paper. I now understood that the whole concept was a dance between the x-variable and the y-variable. The connection between the angle and length of the sides of the triangle revealed themselves to me. This subject is called Trigonometry. Conics was even more fun. Dad made me cut out circles, ellipses and parabolas from coloured charts. We then played games with permutation and combination and probability. Matrices proved to be extremely interesting. I uncovered that matrices is the Science behind animation and graphics. We then stepped into the world of differentiation. We drew curves and made slopes. Hey Presto! The formulae matched with the drawings. Integration worked the other way around. We drew the curves on graph sheets; area under the curve and the formula were in tandem.

Every day was turning out to be more thrilling. I could hardly wait for the evenings. I would sometimes get up in the middle of the night and do Maths problems. Two characters excite me a lot - complex numbers and 'e'. Both these characters give me goosebumps. These perplexing numbers are the very heart of Mathematics. Even concepts like normal distribution curve, Pascal's triangle and harmonic progression are driving me crazy. But in a good way! Life is fun!

I did not spend much time with Chemistry. I know it would be disappointed with me. I only went through the Crash Course in Chemistry on YouTube. It was fantastic.

Physics was more stimulating. The knowledge of where two vectors dot with each other and cross with each other was the aha! moment for me. How distance converted to velocity to acceleration to force to work done to power, sent a chill across my spine. Mr. Ramanan's AhaGuru videos on free body diagrams, tension between pulleys and how to separate a projectile into two separate axis were just too good. Mr. Walter Lewin of MIT was the darling of the lot. His experiments with dipole movements, Van de Graaff, Faraday Cage, friction being independent of mass and surface area, a pendulum and a spring are in a similar to sine wave movement, terminal velocity, operation of the gyroscope and the law of conservation of momentum were touché moments for me. These are some unforgettable experiences in my life.

My dad was "be patient" almost all the time. Just once he got wild with me. He kept demonstrating Avogadro's number and mole concept. After his repeated explanations, when I could not understand this simple concept, he lost his cool.

His elaborate explanation on the importance of each article of the Constitution had a positive effect on me. On the day of the budget my dad took a break from office. My whole world stopped. We were glued to the television screen. Terms like GDP, fiscal deficit, where the money was coming from and was being spent by the government, started to make sense. Dad would not leave me even after the Finance Minister's speech. He surfed channel by channel and made me listen to the reviews of all the analysts. By late afternoon, I had a splitting headache.

Whenever we read the newspapers, I was made to search on Google about the geography and the history behind that event. I wish to mention that my dad, my friend Shiva Shankar and I were finalists in the Trichy quiz. This quiz was conducted by Mr. Ramanan of *The Hindu – Young World fame*. The questions asked by him were out of the world. Sadly, among the six finalists, we came last.

My mother made me watch Simon Sinek's TedTalk. In this talk, Mr. Simon drew three concentric circles. In the outer circle, he wrote 'how'. In the next circle he wrote 'what' and in the inner circle he wrote 'why'. He mentioned that success does not lie in the 'how' and 'what' of things; success lies in asking the question 'why'. Why should I learn Maths? Why should I learn Physics or Chemistry? Why should I learn computers? Why should I learn Economics, budget, History, Geography or our Constitution? Now the whole puzzle seems to make sense. I am itching to go back to school with renewed energy. I regret having wasted 15 years of my life of playing and having fun. I wish I had spent more time with my father, learning from him.

Notes from the parents:

Savitri grew up to be a Maths hater. I was a good student in school. If good meant getting good marks then I was really 'good'. We live in a marks-centric society. I became an engineer without ever relishing or savouring the beauty of Math and Science.

Marks were a result of fear. They were equivalent to surviving in the world.

The trend has not changed in 30 years. We speak to students who score high percentages. How do you use Differentials and Integrals in the real world? How is Matrices connected to the world of computers? What is the difference between a Cross product & a Dot product? Even simple questions like, what is the difference between Distance & Displacement elicit no response.

In school after school, college after college; the story has been the same. When we ask such questions, they maintain 'SILENCE'. We do not want our kid to come up in this marks culture. We want her to *learn Maths and Science for the joy of it.*

If Pappu doesn't get admission into her desired course in our state, she could look for option anywhere in India. If Indian colleges are not willing to admit her, she could look at the colleges across the world as an option to study her desired course. There is room for everyone with a desire and drive.

A frog from the sea visited a well. There it met another frog which enquired where this frog came from. The frog replied – the sea. The well frog probed further – is the sea half as big as the well? The sea frog replied – much bigger! The well frog asked – is the sea at least as big as the well? The sea frog replied – much bigger! The well frog got infuriated and said that 'there can be nothing bigger than the well'.

To us our town is a well, our country is the sea and the world is an ocean. Why not explore the ocean of knowledge, rather than stick to the well of marks?

HEALTH IS WEALTH

I am now becoming a fitness freak. I was not the same a couple of years back.

Initially, I had a craze for Cheetos. Actually, it was not Cheetos but Pokémon and Pikachu. These were the stickers in the pack which attracted me to the product. Then I graduated to Kinderjoy. What lured me to this brand was the toy I used to get along with it. Finally, I settled for Kurkure and Dairy Milk. I would take Rs.50 from my father everyday and buy these things. My mother then scolded my father and ordered him to not give me money anymore. But that was not a problem for me. There were many students who would come to our institute. I would smile at them and make friends. They would take me to the local eateries where I would stuff myself with cakes and pizzas, and then it was Kurkure and Dairy Milk, of course. After sometime, my mother got furious. She reprimanded the students and gave them firm instructions not to treat me. I had to look out for some other source.

My parents would put money in my piggy bank every day. Somedays, they would insert a five rupee coin, at times Rs.10 also. Now my piggy bank was getting full. One day, when my parents were in class, out of sheer desperation, I broke open the piggy bank. There was more than Rs.300 in it. With sheer joy, I went to the nearby grocery store and spent all the money to buy Kurkure and Dairy Milk. I conveniently hid them in a drawer attached to my bed.

When I came back home, I saw my parents sitting on my bed. All the Kurkure and Dairy Milk were on the bed. I confessed and tried to avoid eating junk food from then on, but did not succeed.

One day, we went to a toy store. I chanced upon a Barbie doll set. It was alluring. The Barbie was gorgeous. Her shoes and dresses were appealing. Immediately, I insisted that my parents buy the set. My parents usually don't say no, but this time it was different. Dad and mom said sure in unison. Mom said that to get the set, I had to take up a challenge. For the next 30 days, I had to stop eating Kurkure and Dairy Milk. This was the price I had to pay. I agreed with a heavy heart.

Somehow deep inside, I felt that my parents had planned the whole thing out. To my dismay, they put a chart in my room the next day. It was marked 1 to 30. At the end of 30, the picture of Barbie and her accessories was pasted. The challenge started. The first four days were the most difficult. By the end of the 15th day, I lost interest in these two products. Every day, I put a tick on the chart. I was getting closer and closer to Barbie. I would let out a war cry and do a Maori dance! Then dad would irritate me by telling me that I would lose out and mom would motivate me. I was sure that the two were playing a game with me.

My 30 day challenge got over. The very next day, my parents took me to the toy shop. They gave me the money which I handed over at the counter. Filled with pride, I rushed back to our apartment. I rang every door bell and disturbed all the neighbours to show them the Barbie set.

Afterwards, I lost all interest in chocolates and snacks. My USY had a very strict regimen. I would go to the gym in the morning. I would alternate between cardio on one day and weight training on the next. I would work on all muscle fibres to stay fit.

My schedule consisted of warm-up and pre-stretches for ten minutes. After exercising for nearly an hour, I would do post stretches to strengthen my abdominal muscles. I also loved skipping and would skip at least 100 times twice a week. I also enjoyed the hoola-hoop.

I joined the local zumba course and would dance my heart out thrice a week. Zumba is real fun. On Zumba days, I would go to the gym only to do my post stretch.

I never compromised on my eating. I usually had a hearty breakfast. It consisted of any one of the following: poori, idly, paratha, cornflakes and chocolate milk. I would also regularly have toast bread and omelette. In the afternoon, I would eat a light lunch consisting of a few veggies. Dinner consisted of soup, fruits and boiled vegetables. My mom would give me a concoction of beetroot, nuts, dates, apple and unrefined sugar. It was yucky! I would gobble up two spoons fuls in the morning and night. Mom would urge me to eat fenugreek seeds soaked in water.

Hold it! I sound like an angel. On weekends, when we went to the restaurants, the devil in me would surface. I would attack pizzas, cheese toasts, fried food, jalebis and ice-cream with vengeance. Then I would wait patiently for a whole week to pounce on them yet again.

I just wanted to add one more point. Packaged noodles has always been on my NO list.

In the second half of my USY, I developed a fascination for badminton.

My main inspiration was Balu sir, a thorough gentleman. Whenever I needed help, he would be at my service. He would be at my side till I perfected the shot. Sometimes it would take me an hour, but, Balu sir never got irritated. He's also a tough taskmaster. At times he would make me skip 500 times till I almost dropped dead.

My other source inspiration is Naren, a logistic expert who lives in Singapore. He is short statured but has tremendous stamina and is a regular at the Singapore marathon. Aarthi aunty is yet another hero. She is a beautiful lady in her mid 30s. Aunty practised hard for her mini marathon in Pondicherry where 2000 runners would run by the sea and hardly 100 would make it to the finish. Aunty said, "After the first 10 kilometres, I thought I was going to die. After 15 kilometres, I knew I was going to die. After 19 kilometres, I knew I was dead. After finishing the marathon, I knew that I was so strong that nothing in the world could kill me."

One of the gripping quotes of Jim Rohn is, "Take care of the body it is the only place where you have to live."

Notes from the parents:

As children, we used to play all day long. There were playgrounds everywhere. Now the playgrounds have vanished. The happy and joyful voices of the children have transmuted into gaming sounds. Even during summer holidays, there is silence on the streets.

A doctor once commented, 'the biggest tragedy of the modern society would be, parents seeing their children die before their eyes'. The doctor was indicating at the rampant obesity in India.

On our visit to China, we saw the entire country fit. Government had made exercise compulsory. The Chinese also finished their dinner by 6 pm in the evening. We saw that Singaporeans were *fitness* freaks too and the entire Europe was on the bicycle.

We ensured that academics were not at the cost of health. There is one more mistake that we made. Sagarikka is an athlete and loves basketball, swimming and football. If given a chance to dance, she would do it all day long.

We wish that we had been like Saina Nehwal's parents, who discovered her talents early and supported her in becoming a world-class athlete. But the realisation dawned on us quite late.

What pains us is that most parents let their children sacrifice their sporting skills and *fitness* in the 10th, 11th & 12th standard due to the pressure of academics.

INTO THE WORLD OF COMPUTING

I was bitten by the robot bug. Ever since I saw Rajinikanth's blockbuster 'Robot', I dreamt of making one for myself. Aishwarya Rai was helped by robot Rajinikanth to prepare for her exams. I wanted to make a robot which would also help me with my exams. In my ninth class, I got information that NIT - Trichy was going to conduct a workshop on robotics. So, I bunked school and went for it. To my surprise, I found children from all over Trichy, attending it. I was the only one from my school. They all had teams and I had none. As the workshop proceeded, I had difficulty in assembling my robot and started to cry. The other children started to laugh at my appalling behaviour. Fortunately, the NIT students came to my rescue and the robot was assembled.

Day and night I kept on dreaming about making robots. I asked a Professor what I needed to know to become a robot scientist. He said that I needed knowledge of Matrices, vectors, motors, materials and Java programme. I wanted to learn them all but my tenth standard proved to be a wall between me and my dreams. I had to keep my dreams on a shelf to be explored later on. The opportunity arose with my USY.

Initially, I planned to do some online course in computers but my mom was very particular that I study in some institute. So my search for institutes began. The first institute I went to had no one in it, not even a counsellor. There was an old bald man sitting on the counsellor's desk. He kept picking at the hair in his nostrils as he asked me to fill a register. He said that the counsellor would call me later. Call me! I would never revisit this place even in my dreams. The next place I went to did not even have a counsellor desk. Instead it had a counter like the one you have in the hospitals. Were they going to admit me here? A man spoke to me in broken English and asked me why I wanted to join the course. I spoke to him about my USY. He presumed that I was a school dropout and desperately seeking a computer certificate which would procure me a job and thus get settled in life. The man gave me a lecture on why I should not get disheartened and how learning computers could get me a job which would fetch me a salary of a few thousand rupees. I found the whole episode amusing. Why were these people not listening and trying to find out what I wanted to do? They just assumed what I wanted and started lecturing. I then went to a multimedia centre. A sleepy young lady spat out at me, "Three lakhs." Saying that word would save her time and energy from explaining the whole course. She had already assumed that I would not join.

My mom, on seeing my plight, took me to eQuadriga,a software center. There, I met Mr. Leo Ananth. He is an astute and knowledgeable man. He explained to me that there are two paths to choose from. The programming path which consists of C, C++, Java, Android and Python and the non-programming path which consists of Photoshop, CorelDraw, Flash and Web designing. I enrolled immediately.

On the first day, I was introduced to a calm, beautiful and charming lady. She was Abitha Ma'am. We built an instant rapport and became good friends. She introduced me to C and C++. During tea breaks, we would visit the neighbouring malls and eat cakes and ice creams. This teacher- student bond was a double bond. C programming was full of surprises. Good knowledge of English, helped me comprehend C programming. C++ is an object oriented programming. I was made to understand that this program can be used to make video game and music players. I later learnt that C++ was used for making office applications and operating systems. Chances are Microsoft Windows is written in C++.

Later, I was introduced to the world of Java. My instructor was Ms. Puhal. It was a three month course. Java is simply a list of clear instructions. My primary interest was to create Android applications, for which Java was the doorway. Java is also used in client server web applications.

I also joined an animation course consisting of Photoshop, CorelDraw and Flash. I learnt picture and video editing. I also learnt simple Maths animations with Flash.

Currently I am working on making an application in the Android platform. This application would prove to be useful for students preparing for GRE, SAT, CAT and other competitive exams.

Notes from the parents:

We wish to narrate a couple of incidents on how society poisons the mind of a child. The first one involves a girl in our neighbourhood. She was three years old then. One day, after performing a puja, we offered her prasad. She refused to take the offering from us saying that her God would get angry if she took it and poke her eyes when she went to sleep. How could a three-year-old kid form an opinion and say my God is different from your God?

This incident disturbed us deeply. The society was *colouring* a three year old.

The second incident occurred at a Rotary function, where I was one of the speakers. A 14 year old spoke about not getting admission in a 'good school.' The Principal of that school stated that he would not admit a short, dark complexioned, ugly and poor child. The girl kept crying on stage and wanted to avenge her humiliation. We were rattled that such a young mind could get *coloured* with the thoughts of revenge.

We always dream of the Tagore's world. In his poem he stated "*where the mind is without fear, where the world is not been broken up into fragments by narrow domestic walls... into that heaven of freedom... my Father let my country awake*".

We deliberately avoided sharing our thoughts and prejudices of religion, caste, gender and racial discrimination with Pappu.

Even in our small organisation, a majority of the employees are women. We have people of all religions working with us and till today we have never bothered to know about their castes. At times, as parents we too are tempted to share our negative opinions with her. So far, our child has been *colourless.*

UNDERSTANDING LIFE

Death of a Friend:

Anjana and Subi are my best friends. We used to have regular conference calls during my USY. Occasionally, we would meet at our favourite hideout Dominos Pizza (one of the few places to hang out in my town). Here, we would chat for hours about boys, movies and studies. Hari is my other friend. We would meet in the dance class. Our favourite topics were cricket, football, dance and studies.

An unfortunate incident which occurred during my USY, left a deep impression in my mind. My close friend Gokul met with a car crash along with his brother. They both succumbed to the injuries. Their mother had breathed her last a couple of months before after a bout of illness. I went to pay my last respects to Gokul. It was extremely painful. Their poor father was left with no family. I recalled the words of Arun Rebero uncle, "Life is very short, before you realise it, it gets over. Savour every moment of it, till it lasts." I decided to make the best use of my life because 'Kal Ho Na Ho'.

Death in the Family:

Now I must write about my late grandfather Dr. V.A.Sathgurunath (Pappa). He was an IITian, a footballer and a boxer. He loved Mathematics. He was an expert in steel making and tube technology. He was instrumental in starting the Seamless Steel Tube project at BHEL, Trichy. He also started Jindal Submerged Arc Welding Pipes project at Nashik. He never liked me calling him 'daddu'. He preferred pappa instead. He used to tell me, "I wish to die young, as old as possible." Pappa was a health freak. He used to proudly say I have no ABCD, A is Arthritis, B is Blood Pressure, C is Cholesterol and D is Diabetes.

He trained hundreds of people and got them jobs. Whenever anybody had any financial difficulty, pappa would give them money. This upset me because I knew that they were lying to him, but never did pappa mind. He was a stickler for discipline and used to say, "Everything should be in its place and there is a place for everything." He was another Gandhi in time management. Whenever any staff came late, he would look at the clock and stare at him or her, but he would never say a word. Pappa loved cleanliness. If the drainage got choked, pappa would put his hands inside the drain pipe and clean it. If I vomited, he would collect the vomit in his hands and wash his hand later.

In April 2015, pappa's health started deteriorating. Initially he found it difficult to walk, then he started gasping for breath. Doctors diagnosed that he had COPD[*] (Chronic Obstructive Pulmonary Disorder). He was slowly dying because of difficulty in breathing.

Pappa took it bravely. He knew that his end was near. He lived in another flat in the town. My parents would go and see him every day. I would go and see him daily after the badminton class. He was on oxygen all the time. I would tell him what happened during the day. He enjoyed every bit of what I shared and then I would kiss him and come back home.

On February 7th, 2016 we celebrated his 77th birthday. We hung balloons and festoons. Though pappa could not move his body, he wanted to be well-dressed and clean shaven for the evening. I had the privilege of giving him the shave. He cut a huge cake and we sang songs through the evening. Then we shared good things about pappa. He shed a tear as he knew that he had only few more days to live. On February 13th it was late in the evening. I was waiting to board a bus to Bengaluru, along with Nirmala aunty. I was planning to witness a theatre festival next day. When dad came to the bus depot, I realised something had gone wrong. We rushed to pappa's house. There, right before our eyes he breathed his last. Many people came to pay their last respects. Most of them were the poor ones, whose lives had become brighter because of him. I had now seen death from very close quarters twice in a year. I wish to share a beautiful quote by Paulo Coelho. 'Never. We never lose our loved ones.

They accompany us; they don't disappear from our lives. We are merely in different rooms.'

The Accident:

26th May 2016, is an unforgettable day in my life. It was 1.30 in the afternoon. My parents and I were travelling from Bengaluru to Chennai in our car. A speeding biker veered in front of the car. My mom who was at the wheel, jammed the brake to avoid collision. A truck which had been tailing us rammed our car at the side and our car hit the side railing, spun and halted at the other side of the road.

I was in the backseat, was throw from side to side but was unhurt. My attention first went to my mother who was dazed but conscious. My father was unconscious. Fortunately both of them were wearing their seat belts. The impact of the collision on them was minimal. After a short while, dad regained his consciousness but was in a state of shock.

I was relieved that my parents were fine but also realised that I had to take action as they were in a state of shock. I made my parents sit beside the railings and took the entire luggage out of the car and kept it by the sidewalk. A huge crowd had gathered at the scene by then. I explained to a couple of policemen, who appeared to be taking notes, as to how the accident had occurred. I then called my dad's office and asked our staff Ms.Naveena to inform the insurance and the car service station.

Next I called a couple of key relatives and explained what happened. I also made sure that this information was not shared with other relatives for the time being, as it would create a panic situation.

By now, Mr. Ravi (relative of Ms. Naveena) who works in Hosur (the location of the accident) arrived at the spot. We organised a tow truck and went to the car service centre, where I filled the necessary forms. Then we hired a taxi and took my parents back to Bengaluru.

When the news spread, people started applauding me for the heroic act and said that I had really grown up and matured.

Today, when I look back, I realize that it was the USY which gave me the courage and confidence to face this challenging situation. I am now trained to look for solutions and not the problem.

Friends are good, but family is better:

In this chapter I should have spoken about my parents first. They say 'Parents are the only ones obligated to love you, from the rest of the world, you have to earn it.'

Sometimes I used to take my parents for granted. I would pay no heed to their voice and have regretted it later. Let me share an amusing incident. My mother had gone to Bengaluru. I sat down with dad for the regular 6pm to 10pm schedule. It was my friend Mani's birthday. I compelled my friend along with her brother to accompany me for a night show at a local theater. I was sure that I could convince my father. I approached my father but to my dismay, he asked me to speak to mom who quietly refused. Even though Mani and her group are close friends of our family, mom said that she did not appreciate a night show. Then, I had an emotional hijack. I started wailing and screaming. I banged doors and said nobody in this world loved me. It worked. Dad gave in to the pressure and I went for the movie. It was a terrible movie. A feeling of remorse came over me. I wished I had listened to my parents.

Without my parents, my USY would not have been possible. They were the Producers and Directors of my USY. Every field visit, industrial trip, seminar and class was planned by them. My job was just to execute it.

My dad would spend an hour with me in the morning discussing the newspaper and new words. He diverted his attention from his business to spend the evenings teaching me Math, Physics and Chemistry. He is the reason I started enjoying Maths, Science, Politics, Business, Books and Public Speaking.

My mother is the most beautiful, kindest, patient and balanced human being you will ever meet. Apart from being a business woman, she balances the family, takes care of me, my father and my grandparents. She is also a social activist through the Rotary club. She has conducted blood donation camps and donated artificial limbs through Rotary. She has organised walks to create awareness about Breast Cancer and Autism. She executed a huge project of constructing toilets for girls in a school for the under privileged. Her latest passion is to provide career guidance to the students of under privileged schools.

I have never seen my parents fight with each other. They are my role models.

My father has a fascination for Arnab Goswami (of Times Now fame). This is the only part of him that we dislike. Every evening at dinner time, he switches on the television and forces me to listen to Arnab uncle's lectures. But for that... we seldom watch TV. During my USY, after dinner I would listen to the audios of Antony Robbins or watch some Ted Talks. Mom would share her reading experiences.

This would be followed by answering four question :

1: Was it a Complaint Free Day? To whatever negative thought that came to us about a person or situation, we would say cancel, cancel.

2: Was it a Gratitude Filled Day? Did we say wow and wonderful for the countless miracles that happened in our life? We would thank God for all the wonderful happenings during the day.

3: Was it a Fun Filled Day or did we take our life too seriously? This question helped us to remove stress from our life, so that life would be bright and filled with fun.

4: Was it a Productivity Filled Day? What steps did we take to achieve our goals?

These are the core questions we shared on a daily basis. After we answered the four questions, my parents would go for a walk and I was free for the 'entire evening'.

Notes from the parents:

Doug Wead, the personal assistant to President George Bush said that you can promote anybody but yourself. What this statement meant was if I talked highly of myself, nobody would regard me.

When Savitri talked about herself, she would have no power. But when we talk highly about each other, the power would multiply tenfold.

Sagarikka was another version of Lord Narada, always wanting to play pranks with us. She would go to Savitri and complain about my misgivings, misdoings and eccentricities. She would similarly sit next to me and play the same prank. Little did she know that Savitri and I had a secret pact.

Our strategy was '*Edification*'. '*Edification*' means to instruct or praise someone else other than you. Whenever Sagarikka came to me with a set of complaints about her mother, I would reel out a list of positives about her mother. I would give Pappu a sermon about the greatness of Savitri. And what did Savitri do? She adopted the same strategy.

Realising that her mischief was not working, Pappu had to yield – if you can't beat them, follow them. There was no room for politics now. This does not mean that Savitri and I don't fight, we do have a few but mostly behind closed doors.

As a family we have been totally transparent in all matters. Even before Pappu's USY, we used to discuss personal, business, official and financial matters with her and she would act as our consultant.

By the time she completed her USY, she had matured.

What do you see in this page?

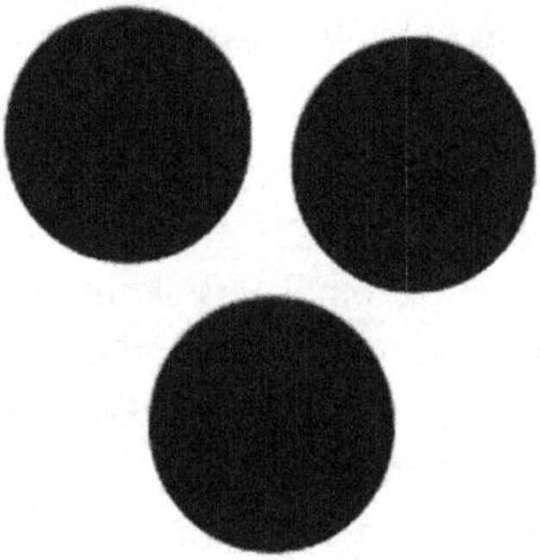

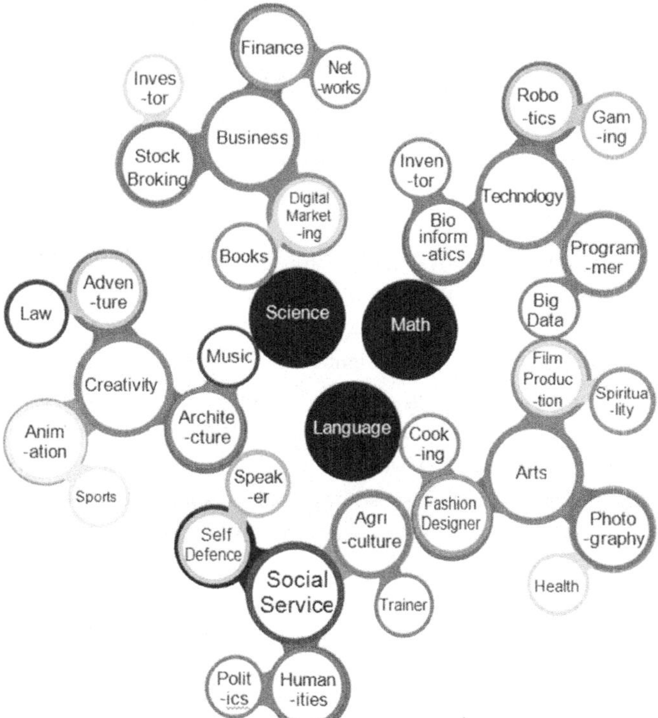

Finance
Net
-works
Inves
-tor
Business
Stock
Broking
Digital
Market
-ing
Books
Robo
-tics
Gam
-ing
Inven
-tor
Technology
Bio
inform
-atics
Program
-mer
Big
Data
Adven
-ture
Law
Science
Math
Music
Creativity
Archite
-cture
Anim
-ation
Sports
Film
Produc
-tion
Spiritua
-lity
Language
Cook
-ing
Arts
Speak
-er
Self
Defence
Agri
-culture
Fashion
Designer
Photo
-graphy
Social
Service
Trainer
Health
Polit
-ics
Human
-ities

CONCLUSION

I showed my friends a page with three black dots and asked them what they saw. My friends replied "Three black dots". They did not focus on the big white space in the background. To me, the three black dots are Maths, Science and Language. I was shown a world beyond that during my USY. A world of business, a world of dreamers, a world of travel and adventure, a world of books, a world of computers, a world of diverse ideas and a world of brilliant minds. I am reminded of Oliver Wendell Holmes's quote 'One's mind, once stretched by a new idea, never regains its original dimensions.'

The USY was also an awakening into the world of Maths and Science. These are the two of the most beautiful subjects in the world. The sheer magic of these subjects made me see that everything around us is a manifestation of these two subjects. If somebody were to ask me, which is more important, Science or worldwide experience, my answer now would be both. They coexist. One cannot be enjoyed at the cost of the other.

Two of my favourite YouTube videos are Ken Robinson's address to RSA on 'Changing Education Paradigms' and Steve Jobs' speech at Stanford. Here are some snippets from the two talks.

Ken Robinson shared a case study. A group of children up to the age of six were asked to list down the advantages of a paper clip. The same activity was then given to children from the age of eight to 12. The final group to do this activity consisted of 14 to 16 year olds. The children of the first group came up with maximum ideas. The oldest group came up with least ideas. Ken Robinson concluded that as we grow old, we grow out of creativity. He says that today's children would retire by 2065. Is the education system equipping the children to handle the problems of 2065? His answer is a stern 'No'. Ken Robinson stated that education teaches us convergence. We also need divergence. I think USY was a year of divergence for me.

Steve Jobs in his address at Stanford said, 'Stay Hungry Stay Foolish'. He insisted that the students should keep searching and never be satisfied.

This search would lead us to our true purpose. The USY was a year of searching for me.

Now I am back in to the world of convergence, into the world of academics. I fully understand that scoring marks is 'important'. Marks are an indication of my competency in the subject. I'm back to school with the realisation that every bit of what I learn is connected to the real world. The world of adventure, fun and travel can wait. In the words of Robert Frost,

> *"The woods are lovely, dark and deep,*
> *But I have promises to keep,*
> *And miles to go before I sleep,*
> *And miles to go before I sleep."*

Please feel free to send me your Comments, Suggestions and Feedback. You can visit me on

Facebook - @sagarikka

Twitter - @sagarikka31

Website - www.sagarikka.com

email - pr@sagarikka.com

DO'S & DON'TS

Dear parents, when we decided to give Sagarikka an year break from school, we followed these guidelines. We prepared a checklist which we thought of sharing with you.

Things to do:

We made a schedule for Sagarikka and she had to adhere to it strictly.

We had to plan her projects, seminars, travel, industrial visits, meeting people at least a month in advance.

We had to fix at least two appointments in a day (especially for sales and interviewing people) so that she could make it to at least one place even if the other appointment got cancelled.

Everyday she had to record her experiences.

We had to encourage her to take risks and were willing to empty our pockets for her to get more experience.

As parents we had to invest at least five hours a day with her to guide her with her studies, reading and even mentoring on day-to-day basis.

We had to consciously protect her from all the negative influence of people. We also had to constantly motivate her when she felt discouraged.

We had to curtail our entertainment. For example. Going to restaurants, watching movies, attending functions etc, to save time and remain focused.

We had to continuously update ourselves and be open minded to learning, going out and talking to people. We also had to follow the routine with her. If she studies, we also study. If she exercises, we also exercise. So the discipline and routine was for all three of us.

Things we avoided:

Watching TV for the sake of entertainment was out of question.

Home was not a place for politics and unnecessary discussion.

Even though Sagarikka took time to get into the groove, we had to be patient. There was no room for criticism.

We avoided giving our opinion at any point and let her make her own decisions.

DIRECT SOURCE OF INSPIRATION

Mr. R. Anbarasu & Krishnan Srinivasan *(SRF group)*

Mr. Arun Rebero *(Conture Solar India Pvt. Ltd)*

Mr. Aswin Sasi Varrier *(Chirst Univ.)*

Ms. Abitha & Ms. Puhal *(eQuadriga)*

Ms. Biju *(Ramyas Hotel)*

Mr. Balasubramanian & Ms. Mala *(Nehru Memorial College, Puttanampatti)*

Dr. Bennett *(National College, Trichy)*

Mr. P.C. Bala *(Author,MatrixBusinessIndiaPvt.Ltd.)*

Ms. Barbara Kozham *(Author)*

Ms. Dhaarini Srinivasan *(ILO - Geneva)*

Ms. Fathima Bathool Maluk *(Master Group of Institutions)*

Mr. Gopalakrishnan *(BHEL)*

Ms. Geetha & Mr. Ramanujan *(Pravaag School, Trichy)*

Mr. Giridhar Raghunathan *(Univ. of Laval)*

Mr. John Benedict *(National Institute for Smart Govt.)*

Judge John D Cunha

Ms. K. Veena & Mr. C.K. Kumaravel *(Naturals)*

Mr. Koushik Raju *(BHUMI)*

Ms. Lisette Gears *(Yoga trainer Amsterdam)*

Mr. Leo Ananth *(eQuadriga)*

Major General Ian Cardozo *(Indian Army)*

Mr. Mahesh Khanna *(Khanna Brothers)*

Mr. Natarajan *(Bank Manager, KVB)*

Mr. Norbo

Mr. Naveen Sivakumar *(Student Architect)*

Mr. Narendra Babu *(Singapore)*

Ms. Padmasini Veerabadran *(Nuremberg - Germany)*

Ms. Priya Vanaraj *(TIME Kids)*

Mr. Rathna Kumar *(Ramyas Hotel)*

Mr. BV Ramanan & Ms. Mythily *(Livia Polymer Bottles Pvt. Ltd)*

Mr. Rahul Ogra *(Mystic Himalayan Trails)*

Mr. Rajesh Parthasarathi *(Baby Industries)*

Ms. & Mr. Ravi Murrugaiah *(Vasan Estates)*

Mr. Ratnesh Mathur *(Aarohi Life Education)*

Dr. Ramakrishnan *(Trust Shantivanam)*

Ms. Radha Natarajan *(LEED)*

Dr. Sherin Kummararaj *(AG Eye Care Hospital)*

Ms. Shanmuga Priya *(Vagus Technologies)*

Mr. Somasundaram *(Amman Steel)*

Ms. Sanjana Ramanan *(Livia Polymer Bottles Pvt. Ltd)*

Mr. Sasi Varrier *(Ashtanga Ayurvedics Pvt. Ltd)*

Mr. Siddharth Joshi *(Blogger)*

Mr. R. Sridharan *(Melbourne University, Australia)*

Mr. Shankar Narayanan *(SPINE Inc. USA)*

Mr. Sasi *(Film Director)*

Ms. Sona Kumaresan *(IIM Ahmedabad)*

Ms. Subhashini & Mr. Manohar *(TATA Hitachi)*

Dr. Uma Arun *(PABCET Group of Institutions)*

Ms. Vanaja Shanmugasundaram *(Naturals)*

Ms. Vrinda Ramanan & Mr. Ramanan *(The Science and Adv. Club, Trichy)*

Mr. Veerasekaran *(BHEL)*

Mr. Vijay Antony *(Actor & Music Director)*

Ms. Vigneshwari Subramanian *(Univ. of Helsinki)*

Mr. A.R. Yoagandran *(Kuviyam Media works)*

Mr. Zarryl Lobo & Mr. Shane Lobo *(Xtra Reinforced Plastics Pvt. Ltd)*

INDIRECT SOURCE OF INSPIRATION

Dr. Abhas Mitra, *(BARC, Mumbai)*

Dr. Archana Sharma *(CERN)*

Mr. Ajay Kaul, *(Jubilant Food work)*

Mr. Alexander MCCall *(Author)*

Ms. Amish Tripati *(Author)*

Ms. Barkha Dutt *(NDTV)*

Mr. Brian Tracy *(Author)*

Ms. Chinmayi *(Playback Singer)*

Mr. Chan Kim *(Author)*

Mr. David Sturt *(Author)*

Mr. Dulat *(RAW Chief)*

Ms. Dipali Sikanad *(Les Conceirges)*

Mr. Frank Bettger *(Author)*

Mr. Gowrishankar *(Author)*

Ms. Jayanthi Natrajan *(Politician)*

Mr. Jack Trout *(Author)*

Ms. Jasumathi Ashra *(Sculpture of hotels)*

Mr. Ken Robinson *(Educationist)*

Ms. Lionel Shriver *(Author)*

Mr. Ninan *(Economic Times)*

Ms. Patricia Narayanan *(Sandeepa Chain of Hotels)*

Mr. N. Ram *(The HIndu)*

Mr. Rostow Ravanan *(Mind Tree)*

Mr. Renee Mauborgne *(Author)*

Ms. Rashmi Bansal *(Author)*

Sadhguru Jaggi Vasudev *(ISHA)*

Mr. Sashi Tharoor *(MP & Author)*

Mr. Sujith Kumar *(Infosys)*

Mr. Subroto Bagchi *(Mind Tree)*

Mr. Simon Sinek *(TED Speaker)*

Mr. Viswanathan Anand *(World Chess Champion)*

Organisations

AMWAY India Pvt. Ltd.

CII

ISHA GROUP

Karnataka High Court

LEED

Network 21

NASSCOM

ORBIT Trichy *(Org. for rehabilitation of the blind in Trichy)*

SHCIL *(Stock Holding Corporation India Limited)*

Shantivanam

TRICHY PLUS

Toastmaster International

The Hindu Lit Fest

Book Club

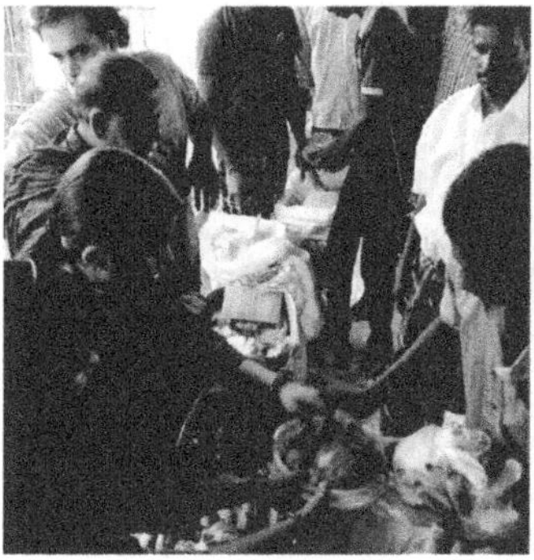

Cuddalore flood relief

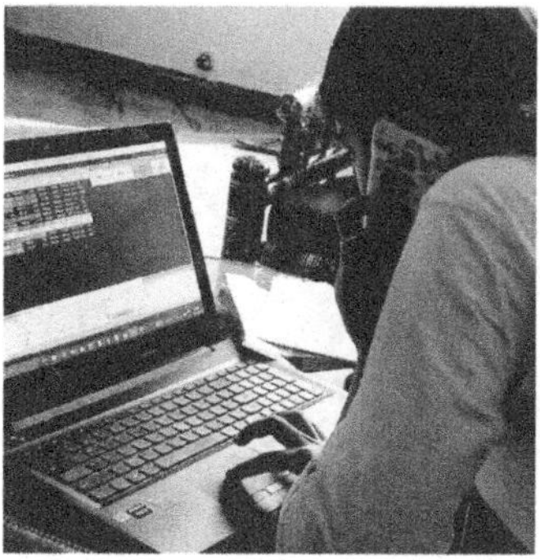

Investing on Stocks

Dr. Bennett - Professor

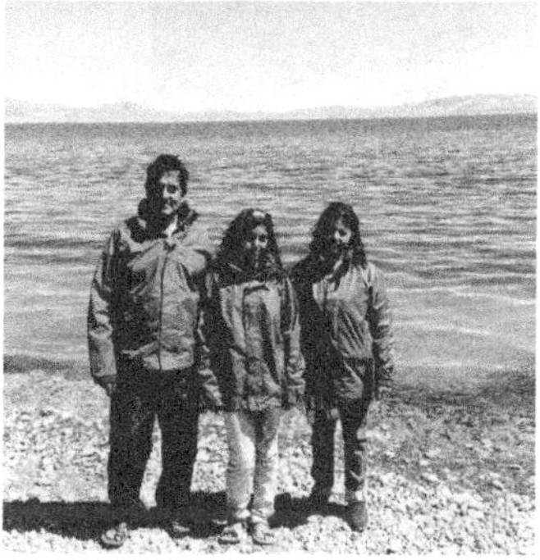

At Lake Manasarovar

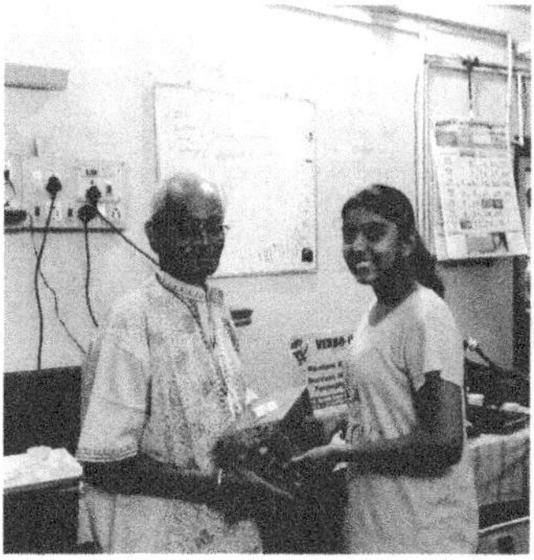

Dr. V. A. Sathgurunath - My Grandfather

At Leh

Major General Ian Cardozo

Mr. Amish Tripathi - Author

Mr. Ajay Kaul - CEO Dominos

Mr. C. K. Kumaravel - CEO Naturals

Mr. Alexander McCall Smith - Author

Mr. Gopalakrishnan - Former Executive Director of BHEL

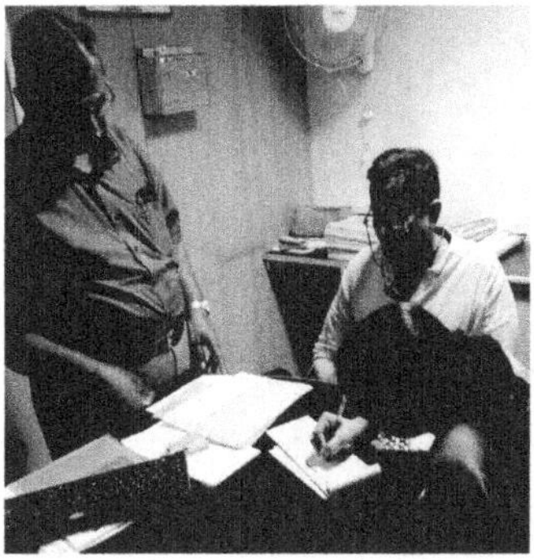

Mr. Natarajan - Karur Vyasa Bank

Mr. Ratnesh - Arohi Open School

Mr. P. C. Bala - Author

Mr. Sasi - Director

Mr. Rajesh - Baby Industries

Mr. Sasi Varrier - Ashtanga Ayurvedics PVT LTD

Mr. Shane Lobo - Xtra Reinforced PVT LTD

Ms. Padmasini - Architect (Germany)

Mr. Shashi Tharoor - Politician & Author

At Mt. Kailash

Ms. Barbara Kozam, Author

Mr. Vijay Antony - Music Director & Actor

Made in the USA
Monee, IL
03 May 2026

49438426R00114